A
MODERN
GUIDE TO
WRITING

THANK-YOU NOTES

HEIDI BENDER

A Modern Guide to Writing Thank-You Notes

Heidi Bender

TABLE OF CONTENTS

INTRODUCTION

QUESTIONS AND ANSWERS

THE EXAMPLES

AT THE OFFICE

FOOD-RELATED

HOLIDAYS

EVENTS

PEOPLE

CONCLUSION

PRAISE FOR A MODERN GUIDE TO WRITING THANK-YOU NOTES

"Modern technology allows us to be impersonal and distant. Heidi's book is an important reminder of the power of a simple written 'thank you' to strengthen our most important relationships."

DAN MILLER, NEW YORK TIMES BESTSELLING AUTHOR,
48 DAYS TO THE WORK YOU LOVE

"Heidi's book is about a topic that is near and dear to my heart, my everyday life, and quite frankly my wallet. The sheer number of relationships I have developed as a result of a simple note is uncountable. The amount of money they have made me is in the hundreds of thousands, if not millions, of dollars. Not to mention they just make me feel good.

  Heidi's book is a must-read for anyone looking to leverage the power of a simple note with two simple words. Read it and you will be forever changed. Apply the principles in this book and you'll be amazed at the results."

MATT MCWILLIAMS, FOUNDER AND PRESIDENT OF MATT
MCWILLIAMS CONSULTING, INC. | *MATTMCWILLIAMS.COM*

"Heidi's book is an amazing guide to writing thank you notes. With her vast examples and tips, you will be able to come up with wording for common thank you note situations."

LISA RYAN, AWARD-WINNING SPEAKER,
AUTHOR AND FOUNDER OF GRATEGY

To my mom, for she taught me to write thank-you notes
before I understood why they are important.

INTRODUCTION

INTRODUCTION

I **HAVE BEEN WRITING THANK-YOU NOTES** since I was very young. As soon as we were old enough to put pen to paper, my mom started the thank-you note writing habit with me and my siblings. We wrote notes for every gift we received from those outside of the immediate family.

If you did not grow up with the tradition of writing thank-you notes, it is very possible that you have never written one. My husband's family did not grow up writing them. Mine did. I learned how to write them. He didn't. That's okay! Don't feel intimidated if this is a new habit. It is never too late to start the tradition for yourself and with your family.

While there are many ways to send your thanks (in fact, I've written an entire chapter dedicated to various methods, including email, in person, on the phone, or via social media), I recommend handwriting thank-you notes in most situations, as they are more personable and memorable. Writing a thank-you note is easy once you do it a few times—and getting started is very simple. Buy a box of note cards. Write them. Address and stamp them. Mail them.

Here are a few more things to remember:

- **Start with a nice pen.** Nice does not mean expensive. However, do not use a super cheap pen that you got for free somewhere. It very likely will not write well and may leave behind ugly ink blobs. I prefer to write with a fine point pen, but you can use whatever point you prefer.

- **You will also need stamps, address labels, and note cards** (if you are sending it via mail). My recommendations for thank-you note brands can be found on the resources page at *www.tonsofthanks.com*.

- **The receiver may never acknowledge the thank-you note. That's okay.** Remember that you are writing the note to express your gratitude or acknowledge a gift.

- **A thank-you will be memorable if it is personal.** The recipient may even be touched simply by the fact that you sent one. Maybe they have never or rarely are thanked for what they do.

Of course, there's the matter of what to write. Sometimes, knowing what to say in a note can feel very challenging. That's why I've created this book. The examples here can be used for inspiration. Some sections will also have templates and tips specific to a particular topic. You can pick and choose, mix and match from these examples to create the message you want. My hope is that this book will help you become confident in writing thank-you notes.

WHY WRITE A
THANK-YOU NOTE?

ONE OF THE GREATEST PLEASURES in life is giving and receiving. Most people like to receive gifts or help others with something. We are often quick to reply with a verbal "Thanks" or "Thank you" in person. We've said these responses so many times they've almost lost their meaning. They've become an automatic response. A thank-you note will make your thanks/appreciation/gratitude feel meaningful.

Let's take a look at the top reasons for writing and sending a thank-you note:

SHOW YOUR GRATITUDE!

The #1 reason to write a thank-you note is to show your gratitude. If you received a gift or some help with a situation, let the giver/helper know how much you appreciate it with a thank-you note.

It's very important to remember that we are not entitled to gifts. We may feel like we are entitled to gifts for certain milestone events like graduations, first baby, and weddings. However, how people decide to spend their money or time is up to them. Remember that it is THEIR money that they are choosing to give to YOU. Giving a gift is rarely, if ever, required. If your attitude is not an attitude of gratitude, you many not receive any gifts again.

ACKNOWLEDGE THE TIME, THOUGHT, AND EFFORT THAT WENT INTO THE GIFT.

Gift givers like to be recognized for their efforts. It's possible that a great deal of thought went into the picking out of the gift; or that the person may have had to sacrifice something else in their budget in order to give you something nice.

Perhaps, you've given someone a gift for one or more of these events and didn't receive a thank-you note. How did that make you feel? Some people I've encountered brush it off, saying they do not expect them anymore. I can see disappointment in their eyes. There are others that have never received a thank-you note ever. Make their day by sending them a note!

It is important to remember, however, that some people will not acknowledge your note. That's not the point of writing one. This does not mean your note did not make them feel recognized and appreciated.

BUILD RELATIONSHIPS

Writing a thank-you note also allows you to continue building a relationship with the person who gave you the gift. It becomes another point of contact. This can work very well for business contacts. The thank-you note can be to thank them for meeting you for lunch or a phone conversation. The thank-you note could also be used as an opportunity to include an invitation to get together again.

SHOW HOW THE GIFT IS BEING USED

If you received a gift that changed your life, definitely write the person a thank-you note to let them know. The impact may not be realized right away. So this could be your second thank-you note as hopefully you thanked them for the gift when you received it.

This type of gift could be a large sum of money that allowed you to do something otherwise not possible (or at least not as quickly). Perhaps, a down payment for a house.

Or what about a life-changing book? For example, I've given Dave Ramsey's *The Total Money Makeover* book as a wedding gift. The couple's finances may be in order, but what if they are not? What if they read the book and follow its advice which then has a profound positive impact on their finances? It would be nice to hear about that, even if it is many years later.

FEELING THANKFUL FOR THE
GOOD THINGS IN YOUR LIFE

Thank-you note writing can also be lesson in gratitude. When you write a thank-you note, you stop focusing on yourself and remember what the other person has done for you. It's an opportunity for you to feel grateful, to appreciate what and who you have in your life.

IT'S FUN!

Some people find great joy in writing thank-you notes to someone. From picking out the card to finding the perfect stickers to put on the envelope (when appropriate). There is pleasure in browsing card designs and choosing a card that will be well liked by the recipient.

A handwritten thank you takes effort and giving one to someone could make their day. When a thank-you note shows up in someone's mailbox or on their desk, it is very likely the only note of thanks they receive that day. It will put a smile on their face. People like to be recognized for their efforts.

And, of course, it is polite to send a thank-you note!

ABOUT THE EXAMPLES AND WORDING USED IN THIS BOOK

BEFORE WE DIVE INTO THANK-YOU NOTE templates and examples, there are a few things I want you to keep in mind.

This book contains many thank-you note examples. These examples can be used as inspiration for your own thank-you notes. These examples are written in my words. My words may not match your writing or talking style. If my examples do not fit you or your situation exactly, feel free to modify them. Please use the examples as a guide and make changes as you prefer for writing thank-you notes.

Some examples will include items in [brackets]. In these examples, you will need to replace what is in the brackets with your own words. For example: *Thank you for the [Gift]*. In your note, replace "Gift" with the item you received. Example: "Thank you for the cookbook."

You can also take sentences from different thank-you note examples to put together a version specific to your situation. If you like part of an example, you can try browsing other sections in the book for inspiration for that second or third sentence.

After reading an example, you may think, "I would never say that!" That's fine. We all have our own way of talking and preferred word choices. My goal is to provide examples that are not cheesy or corny. I've only included examples that I would use in my own life. Therefore, I've avoided poems and rhymes, such as "Thanks a bunch for the lunch."

Also, I will not ever use "I can't thank you enough" in an example. I understand the intention (very thankful), but what is enough? What would it take to thank someone "enough"? Why do your thanks not measure up? There likely will not be a monetary value or any other value that can be "enough."

Your words will be "enough." Enough is giving proper thanks.

Alternatives to "I can't thank you enough" are:

- *I appreciate how much you've done for me because [insert specific reason].*

- *I'm very grateful for all of your help. Your help with [how they helped] got me out of the bind I was in!*

- *How can I thank you?*

If you want to go beyond a thank-you note and do a something extra for them, consider thanking them with a gift. Perhaps, a gift card to their favorite store or a restaurant.

I have also avoided "It will come in handy" when referring to a gift. This is because I used this sentence many times as a child when I wrote a thank-you after receiving money from my great aunts and uncle. The note went like this many times:

Thank you for the money. I really appreciate it. It will come in handy.

I had no idea what I would be spending the money on, and most of it was put into my savings account. I didn't know how it would be handy! Not using "It will come in handy" is a personal choice on my part. If you like the phrase, you can use it.

USING ADJECTIVES

One easy way to modify an example is to add or change the adjectives to your liking. I recommend never using a word that you would not say in your life. Don't say "totally awesome" if you never say "awesome." Think about words that are complimentary to the gift.

You can also use a thesaurus to come up with words. However, if you want to write thank-you notes quickly, I suggest using words you already are comfortable saying rather than spending time looking for that perfect word.

"THANK YOU" ALTERNATIVES

Saying "Thank you for the [item]" is a very common phrase in thank-you notes. This phrase is fine to use, but if you want to mix it up, you can replace "Thank you for..." with one of these alternatives:

- I am grateful for…
- I appreciate…
- Your generosity…
- I am thankful for…

In short, there is no wrong way to say thank you. The important thing is that you do so in a way that is personal and meaningful to you and to the person to whom you're sending the note.

HOW TO WRITE A THANK-YOU NOTE

HERE IS A BASIC OUTLINE for a thank-you note that can be used for most occasions.

> [1]*Dear* [insert name of gift giver],
>
> [2]*Thank you for the* [Insert the gift]. [3][Insert specific detail about the gift that you liked or why you liked it]. [3a][Insert optional one or two sentences about the gift or seeing the person again, etc.]
> [4]*Closing,*
>
> [5][Sign your name]

If you look closely at the example above, you'll notice that there are five key components of a great thank-you note:

1. The Greeting: Dear [insert name of gift giver],

2. The Thank You: Thank you for the [Gift].

3. The What or Why: [Insert specific detail about the gift that you liked or why you liked it].

   a. [Insert optional one or two sentences about the gift or seeing the person again, etc.]

4. Closing: Cap off your note with a closing salutation.

5. Signature: Sign your name.

Let's take a closer look at each one.

1. The Greeting. The first step is to address the person. This can be done with *Hi*, *Hello*, or *Dear,* followed by their name. Alternatively, you can use only their name.

2. The Thank You. Next, write what you are thanking them for. If it was a gift, refer to it specifically. If someone helped you with something, mention how they helped. This can be done in one sentence. I encourage you to not be overly creative. Do not make up cheesy rhymes. This may feel fun when making it up, but it will very likely come across as cheesy or corny to the recipient.

3. The What or Why. Describe how you will use the gift, why you like it, or compliment it. If you have already used it, tell the person how you used it. If you are writing a thank-you note for money, say how you spent the money or what you are saving it for. This section can be one or two sentences, and it will make the gift giver feel appreciated.

4. Closing. This is where you say *Love*, *Sincerely*, or my personal favorite, *Thanks Again!* There are other choices such as *Best Regards, Regards, Kind Regards, All the best*, etc. The option that you choose will depend on your relationship with the person and your personality.

5. Signature. Sign your name. If you are writing the thank-you note on behalf of your family, you can sign everyone's names.

This basic structure is a fit for nearly all occasions. As long as your note includes these five components, you're good to go.

TWO THANK-YOU NOTE TEMPLATES

THESE TWO TEMPLATES can be used for nearly every gift or situation.

The first template is the same as the example we just discussed. It starts with, "Thank you for the…" This is an easy way to start the thank-you note as it mentions the gift from the start. The second template requires a bit more creativity.

Below, you will find four thank-you note examples written using both templates. I hope they will inspire the wording you choose for thank-you notes.

Aim for three or four sentences. Thank-you notes that are less than three sentences may feel too short or incomplete to the reader. If you are stumped, or if three sentences are not practical for your situation, write the note anyway. A short note is better than no note!

Template #1: Starting with "Thank you"

Dear [insert name of gift giver],

Thank you for the [Insert the gift]. [Insert specific detail about the gift that you liked or why you liked it]. [Insert optional one or two sentences about the gift of seeing the person again, etc.]

[Insert closing],

[Sign your Name]

Template #2: Starting with Something Else

The first sentence will be the most challenging. Think about where you received the gift, or start with a compliment. Also, the order of the sentences in the templates can sometimes be arranged so that the "thank you" is in the last sentence.

Dear [insert name of gift giver],

[Insert a first sentence suggestion from below list or devise your own]. *I* [appreciate, am thank for, etc.] *the* [Gift]. [Insert specific detail about gift that you liked or why you liked it].

[Insert closing],

[Sign your Name]

First Sentence Suggestions:

- *I enjoyed seeing you at* [where you saw them].

- *I had a great time visiting with you at* [where you were].

- *Your* [item, such as cakes] *are always wonderful!*

- *The* [item, such as a book] was *awesome!*

LET'S TAKE A LOOK AT A FEW EXAMPLES...

These examples are intended to be used as a guide only. They should help you get started. The four examples below will be written twice to provide an example of each template.

Example #1 (Template #1): Cookbook as Gift

Dear Alice,

Thank you for the cookbook. I like that it includes pictures for most of the recipes. I've already made the recipe for chicken pot pie and loved it!

Thanks Again!

[Your Name]

Example #1 (Template #2): Cookbook as Gift

Dear Alice,

I enjoyed seeing you last weekend at the family get together. I was surprised to receive a cookbook from you! I like that it includes pictures for most of the recipes. Thank you for sharing this resource with me.

Thanks Again!

[Your Name]

Example #2 (Template #1): Money as Gift

Money is one of the most popular gifts received at weddings, graduations, and birthdays. Be sure to indicate your plans for the money in the thank-you note. More examples can be found in the Money and Gift Cards section of this book.

NOTE: You do not need to include the amount given in your note. If the money was received in the mail, writing a thank-you note is particularly important as it lets the giver know you have received it.

> *Dear Mr. and Mrs. Jones,*
>
> *Thank you for attending our wedding. We also appreciate your generous gift. We will be using it towards the purchase of a new couch. We enjoyed visiting with you and look forward to seeing you again soon.*
>
> *Sincerely,*
>
> [Your Name]

Example #2 (Template #2): Money as Gift

> *Dear Mr. and Mrs. Jones,*
>
> *We were excited to see you at the wedding and enjoyed visiting with you. We appreciate your generous gift. We will be using it towards the purchase of a new couch. We look forward to seeing you again soon.*
>
> *Sincerely,*
>
> [Your Name]

Example #3 (Template #1): Help Received

This example is for when someone helps you out. This could be a co-worker at your job, a family member, a friend, someone at your church, etc.

> *Dear Jake,*
>
> *Thank you for helping me with that difficult project last week. I greatly appreciate your help in finding the solution. Working with you saved me significant time and we were able to meet the customer's due date.*
>
> *Best regards,*
>
> [Your Name]

Example #3 (Template #2): Help Received

Dear Jake,

Working with you saved me significant time last week! Thank you for helping me with that difficult project. I greatly appreciate your help in finding the solution and that we were able to meet the customer's due date.

Best regards,

[Your Name]

Example #4 (Template #1): Help Received

Dear Thomas,

Thank you for painting my garage for me last week. It looks great and now I will not need to worry about the wood being damaged from snow this winter. Thank you for taking the time to help me. See you soon!

Sincerely,

[Your Name]

Example #4 (Template #2): Help Received

Dear Thomas,

My garage looks great! Thanks for painting it last week. I am also happy that I will not need to worry about the wood being damaged from snow this winter. Thank you for taking the time to help me. See you soon!

Sincerely,

[Your Name]

THE ONE-SENTENCE THANK-YOU NOTE

GENERALLY, I RECOMMEND including at least 2 or 3 sentences in a thank-you note. The examples and templates in this book follow that format. However, sometimes a one sentence thank-you can be appreciated just as much as a longer thank-you note.

If you can only think of one sentence to say, write it! It is better than not expressing your thanks at all. Don't let "I don't know what to say" be your excuse. "*Thank you for the* [fill in blank]" or, "*Thanks for* [fill in blank]," is all you need. Fill in the blank with the gift, help, situation, or for whatever it is that you are thankful.

A one sentence thank you can be meaningful at the work place. The one sentence thank you could also be used on social media.

At my office job, I've received only a few messages in an instant message that stood out and felt meaningful. "I appreciate your time" made me feel so much more thanked than a quick "Thanks" ever could. Receiving a message with "Thanks" or "Thank you" has happened so often that it doesn't feel meaningful anymore. The more thoughtful message, short as it was, made me feel that this person was truly thankful that I had spent a few minutes on a task for them.

One day I came to my desk and found an index card that said, "Thanks for always making me feel better about being new." The note was from a newer employee that I was mentoring. Knowing that she appreciated the time I was spending with her made my day.

Examples:

> *Thank you for helping me out today!*
>
> *I appreciate all the time you spend answering my questions!*
>
> *Thanks for the Valentine's Day treat!*
>
> *Lunch was great today. Thanks!*
>
> *Thank you for sharing your tips with me.*
>
> *I am grateful to you for covering for me while I was out sick.*
>
> *Thank you for taking me out to lunch.*
>
> *Thanks for taking the time to help me.*
>
> *I appreciate your time spent reviewing my work.*
>
> *Thanks for stepping in on that conference call when I wasn't sure of the answers.*

HOW TO WRITE YOUR OWN THANK-YOU NOTE WITHOUT EXAMPLES

ONE CHALLENGING ASPECT of writing thank-you notes is coming up with what to say in the note. Examples of thank-you note wording can help but what if you don't like any of them? Here are some questions to consider:

- Why are you thanking the person?

- What would you say to them in person?

- What can you add that will be unique and remarkable and make them want to keep the card?

The thank-you note should be:

- Honest.

- Specific.

- Accurate.

- Personal. It should not feel generic.

- In your own words. No fancy adjectives that you found in a thesaurus or adjective list.

- Appealing to an emotion.

Another method that can be used to come up with thank-you note wording is sentence completion exercises. Sentence completion exercises can help you focus and organize your thoughts. The result can be used to write a meaningful thank-you note in your own words.

Complete one or more of the following sentences regarding why you will be writing the thank-you note. This could be a gift, act of service, for dinner, etc. In the examples below, substitute "gift" with what is appropriate for the thank-you note situation.

Pick one, two or three sentences that seem easy to answer. Then use your responses to help write the thank-you note. I will demonstrate with a few examples:

- *I am thankful for the gift because...*

- *The person helped me with....*

- *The event was meaningful because...*

- *I am thankful for the act of service because....*

- *When I received this gift I felt...*

- *The reason I appreciate this gift is...*

- *I will spend the money I received on...*

- *I will save the money I received for...*

- *What I liked best about this gift is....*

- *One more thing I liked....*

SENTENCE COMPLETION EXAMPLES

Example #1

For this example, I will pretend that I received a cat T-shirt as a gift from my friend, Alice.

- I am thankful for the gift because. . .<u>I love cats</u>.
- What I liked best about this gift is. . .<u>The design on the T-shirt and the pretty color</u>.

The Thank-You Note:

Dear Alice,

Thank you for the cat t-shirt. I like the unique design and I'm happy to add another cat t-shirt to my collection. Also, choosing purple as the color was perfect for me!

Thanks again!

Heidi

Example #2

My grandma, who gifted me $50 for my birthday

- I am thankful for the gift because. . .<u>Having a bit of extra money is fun to spend</u>.
- When I received this gift I felt. . .<u>Excited to spend it</u>.
- I will spend the money I received on. . .<u>A new swimsuit</u>.

(Remember when writing a thank-you note for money, the amount does not need to be mentioned.)

The Thank-You Note:

> *Hi Grandma,*
>
> *Thank you for the birthday money! I am excited to spend it on a new swimsuit. I've had my eye on one for a while. I hope to see you soon.*
>
> *Love,*
>
> *Heidi*

Example #3

My friend, Ann, who brought me food after my surgery

- The person helped me with. . .<u>Meals</u>.
- The event was meaningful because. . .<u>I didn't have to worry about cooking</u>.
- I am thankful for the act of service because. . .<u>I was unable to do it myself</u>.

The Thank-You Note:

> *Dear Ann,*
>
> *I am very glad that I did not have to worry about cooking after my surgery. I was not able to stand long enough to make anything for a few days. Thank you so much for bringing over 2 casseroles. The egg and sausage one was fantastic for breakfast. The kids also loved the lasagna casserole. We enjoyed your cooking.*
>
> *Best regards,*
>
> *Heidi and the kids*

Example #4

My boss, Bob, who took me to a networking event.

- The event was meaningful because. . .<u>I met many new contacts in the industry. I made two appointments for lunch next week with potential new customers. The company finds value in networking</u>.

The Thank-You Note:

Dear Bob,

Thank you for taking me to the networking event at Local Convention Center last week. I enjoyed meeting new contacts in our industry. I also was able to set up two lunches with people interested in our product! I am pleased that our company appreciates the value of networking in person. I am already looking forward to the next event!

Sincerely,

Heidi

Try these sentence completion exercises next time you find yourself stuck in thank-you note writer's block!

THANK-YOU NOTE WRITING TIPS

HERE ARE SOME TIPS to help you with thank-you note writing.

1. **Specifically mention the gift and include a detail about it.** This is the #1 tip for a great thank-you note. This acknowledges the gift and shows your appreciation. The detail will be what makes the thank-you note great. It will give the thank-you note a genuine feeling. The note will not feel generic, or like an example copied from the Internet or a book.

2. **Handwrite the note.** This will make the thank-you note stand out. It will feel more personal and will be remembered. Email is easy, but most people will appreciate the extra time and effort you took to handwrite the note. People also like to get something other than bills in the mailbox!

3. **Be yourself when writing the thank-you note.** Only use words that you would use in your own life. If you copy an example with adjectives you'd never use, the recipient may sense this when reading it. They may think you copied the note from somewhere!

4. **Handwrite their address on the envelope.** Address labels are fine for the return address label only. A handwritten address usually indicates to the receiver that this is not a bill or junk mail.

5. **Send the note promptly, as soon as possible after receiving the gift.** Within a week is a good timeline to aim for.

6. **Think about what you'd like to see in a thank-you note written to you.** Include something similar when writing your thanks.

7. **Do not write with a cheap pen that leaves behind ink blobs.**

8. **Use a quality thank-you note card.** This is a note card where you cannot see through the envelope or the card. My recommendations can be found on the Resources page at www.tonsofthanks.com.

9. **Keep a box of thank-you notes on hand.** That way you will be ready when you need to write a note.

10. **Spell the recipient's name correctly.** For example, is there one or two L's in their spelling of Michelle?

11. **Make thank-you note writing a habit by sending them consistently.**

12. **Sending a thank-you note late is better than not sending one at all!**

13. **If you struggle to have legible handwriting, try writing slower.**

14. **If you do not know where to send a thank-you note, ask the recipient for their address.** Or see following chapter on how to find addresses.

15. **Use stickers for informal thank-you notes to give the envelopes some personality!** I love cat stickers and use them often. However, it's important to keep the recipient in mind when choosing embellishments. I do not use cat stickers when I know the recipient does not like cats.

16. **When you receive multiple gifts from the same person at the same time, mention each gift in the thank-you note.**

17. **Think of thank-you note writing as a way to bless others!** Receiving a note from you may make their day.

18. **Make sure you select the correct postage.** Remember, some thank-you note cards have a non-standard envelope size. In the United States, the postage rate is a bit higher. Check with your local post office or on the USPS website. Other countries may also have different rates based on the envelope dimensions.

19. **Your note can do double-duty.** If your birthday is close to a holiday where gifts are given, you can write one thank-you note for the birthday gifts and holiday gifts to those that gave you a gift for both!

20. **You can send one note on behalf of multiple people.** Twins (while still living at home together), can use the same thank-you note card when both twins received a gift at the same time (birthdays, graduation, etc.). However, they should each write their own note inside the card.

QUESTIONS AND ANSWERS

Q&A:
HOW DO I CHOOSE THE DESIGN OF A THANK-YOU CARD?

IF YOU CHOOSE TO SEND a handwritten thank-you note, there are thousands of options for thank-you cards. In fact, there are so many choices that it may feel overwhelming when you need to pick out a card to send to someone. Look for cards that are blank on the inside, so you can want to write your own message. Here are tips that will help you make your decision:

1. **A classic "Thank You" on the front of the card will work for all occasions.** These are solid color cards (usually white), with only "Thank You" written on the front of the card and nothing else. No other design. They may look basic, but they will convey your gratitude. This is a good choice if you feel overwhelmed with the number of choices.

2. **Pick a theme that you like!** The cards may or may not have "Thank You" on the outside. I love cats, so I enjoy sending cat-themed thank-you notes. If there is a theme you really like, use it—but be sure to be

mindful of your recipient. If you know they hate cats, then it's best to choose a card that doesn't include cats.

3. **Pick a theme that the receiver likes!** My oldest sister loves birds. When I send her a thank-you note, I try to find a pretty bird design. If you know the receiver well, go with something that you know they will like. They will appreciate that you chose a card with them in mind.

4. **Remember to be kind to the color blind.** If you are sending a note to someone that is color blind, it is best to stick with a white card and dark ink. This will guarantee that they will be able to read it! I once sent my dad (he is color blind) a thank-you note on a dark purple note card written with a pen that used silver ink. My mom had to read it to him! There was not enough contrast between the color of the paper and the ink for him to be able to see the words. Oops!

5. **Choose a design that will become associated with you.** Another option is to choose one design that you like very much and use it for every thank-you note that you send. If it has a distinctive envelope design, people will know it is from you as soon as they see it in their mailbox! If you write thank-you notes to your co-workers and they post it near their desk, others will know who sent the note just by seeing it. This options also works if you feel like there are too many choices. Find one that you like and stick with it. This eliminates the time and energy needed to review options in the future.

6. **Choose a card themed for your event.** Getting married? Choose a wedding themed thank-you note. Having a baby shower? Go with a baby shower theme. Graduating from high school or college? Pick a graduation theme or a card with your school logo.

7. **Pick your favorite color.** My favorite color is purple, so I tend to favor purple note cards. The purple could be the "Thank You" on a classic thank-you card, or the actual card may be purple.

8. **Don't choose a card at all.** You can use a blank piece of paper or an index card. Even a sticky note will work for a short one-sentence thank-you note being left on the desk of a co-worker.

Q&A:
HOW DO I FIND THE
ADDRESSES I NEED?

To MAIL A THANK-YOU NOTE, you will obviously need the recipient's address—but finding their address can feel painful, time consuming, and frustrating. I have several suggestions to help you find addresses as quickly as possible.

- **Ask the recipient for their address.** This may be the fastest way to obtain an address. You can ask them in person, in an email, text message, Facebook message, or however you usually communicate them.

- **Use a free online address book.** Postable.com offers a free online address book. Once you register with them (which is free as of writing this book), you can share the link with your friends and family and ask them to input their own addresses.

If you do not want to ask, do not have the opportunity to ask, or want the thank-you note to be a surprise, try one these methods:

- **Check your address list for weddings, graduations, baby showers, or another event where invitations were mailed.** If the recipient attended an event you hosted, you likely already have their address. Also, if you had people sign a guest list book at your wedding reception, the guest book may have included a column for an address. Even if it didn't, some people might have written in their address anyway.

- **Ask your Mom, other relative or a friend if they have the address.** My mom is an excellent resource for family member addresses.

- **Check your address book.** Perhaps you already have it! When I moved out, my mom gave me an address book filled with addresses of relatives and friends.

- **Check the phone book.** This works if the person still has a land line phone and lives in the same area as you.

- **You can try looking online, but only use the address if you are 100% sure the address listed is correct.** You do not need to go to the extent of paying for an address finder service.

- **Look in your church directory.** This is a great resource if your church had a wedding or baby shower for you, especially if the event was announced via a bulletin and invitations were not mailed to attendees.

- **If the person has a blog, subscribe to their newsletter as their address may be in it.**

- **Once you determine their address, be sure to use a return address label when you mail the thank-you note.** This way, the recipient will have the opportunity to record your address in their address book.

NOTE: I don't recommend asking co-workers for their home addresses unless it is someone you know well, as requesting it could feel invasive. If you want to handwrite them a note, hand it to them or leave it on their desk. Otherwise, opt for emailing your coworker.

Sometimes, after your due diligence, you may not be able to obtain an address. Or a person doesn't want to give out their address. In these situations, you can hand deliver the thank you, send them a thank-you email, thank them in person, call them on the phone, or send them a text. Usually, a handwritten thank-you note is recommended, but a thank you in an email or Facebook message is better than no thank-you note at all!

Q&A:
WHAT IS THE BEST WAY
TO DELIVER THE
THANK-YOU NOTE?

THERE ARE MANY WAYS to tell someone thank you. Usually, I prefer a handwritten thank-you note (reasons discussed below). Other options include email, social media, text message, on the phone, in person, and online services. All have their place.

Ultimately, you will need to decide which method is right for your situation, knowing that sometimes people will disagree with your choice. Also, at times, more than one method can be used. For example, you can send a handwritten thank-you note immediately after you receive a gift. Then follow up with another method with a picture of you using the gift.

THE HANDWRITTEN THANK-YOU NOTE

Handwritten thank-you notes can have several advantages over other methods of saying thank you. First, you spend extra time to choose a card and handwrite it. Most people appreciate this effort and are also pleasantly surprised when they find anything handwritten in their mailbox. Do you remember the last time you received a handwritten letter or note?

Handwriting the note also forces you to slow down and choose your words carefully. There is not a backspace key. Once the words are on paper, they are permanent.

The recipient may also display the thank-you note card on their desk or perhaps, on a bulletin board in their office. The note card becomes a physical reminder of your gratitude.

If you are thinking no one writes thank-you notes anymore, there is plenty of evidence to the contrary. There are many card companies that still sell thank-you note cards. Take a look the next time you are at a major retail store. Their card section very likely has boxes of thank-you note cards. If no one bought cards, companies would stop selling them.

NOTE: if you have a condition (arthritis, disability, other hand issues, etc.) that leaves you unable to write, please use whatever method you can to thank someone. The encouragement to write handwritten notes is intended for those that are physically able to handwrite.

IN PERSON

When someone hands you a gift or does something for you, you can tell them "thanks" on the spot. I often do this when someone helps me with a problem at the office. The verbal thanks can feel very casual, however. Saying "thanks" or "thank-you" has become an automatic response. If I am thanking someone in person, I try to personalize it just a bit more by saying how he or she specifically helped me. For example: "You really saved me a lot of time."

INSTANT MESSAGING

At my office, we use instant messaging software to communicate throughout the day. While receiving instant messages can often feel like an interruption, it's nice when the message includes a thank you! Sending a full length thank-you note in an instant message may feel awkward, so I would recommend sending an email or handwriting a note if you have a lot to say. However, a quick "Thank you!" message sent immediately after someone does something for you will likely be appreciated.

TEXT MESSAGING

A thank you can be sent very quickly with a text message, if you know the person's mobile phone number. You can also send a picture of the gift you received in action (when applicable). For example, if someone gave your child an outfit, you could send them a picture of the child wearing the outfit.

Also, a text message thank you is useful for less formal gifts or occasions. Perhaps, a friend decided to treat you to lunch. If it is a friend you see often, you could send a thank-you text. If someone gave you a gift card to a restaurant, you can send them a text with a picture of what you ordered.

EMAIL

If you do not know someone's home (or office) address and do not feel comfortable asking for it, sending an email thank you is an option. Also, if email is your primary way of communicating with someone, thanking them via an email can be a good choice.

Email works well in office settings where you would prefer

to not hand deliver a written thank-you card to them, or if the person works in a different location.

However, if someone is in a different office location, they may be impressed if you took the time to find their office address. When I was Employee of the Month, I wanted to thank the vice-president who was responsible for the monetary award that came with the title. She works from her home office in a different state. To surprise her, I was able to get her address from her assistant. Her assistant later told me that the vice president was very impressed that I mailed a thank-you note. I have a feeling she doesn't get very many thank-you notes from other Employee of the Month recipients.

Email can also be used when sending a thank-you note following a job interview. For some interviews, a handwritten thank-you note is going to be best. Please refer to the job interview section for tips on when to mail vs. email the note.

AUTOMATED THANK-YOU EMAILS

Businesses may send out automated emails after a visit or a purchase. For example, I receive an automated thank-you email from my veterinarian's office after I take a cat in for a check. I suppose this is nice in a way, but after you get a few of them, they feel a bit meaningless. They look and feel automated.

Sure, it's nice to get an automated thank-you email, but with people receiving more emails than ever before in history, the thank-you note email may never be read. And it may not make the customers feel appreciated when it's obviously automated. One way to make it feel less automated (while still using a form) is to include the person's name, name of pet, what was purchased, etc.

PHONE

Calling someone on the phone and thanking them is another option. With email, text messaging, and social media, phone calls happen less and less. I do not recommend leaving your "thank you" in a voice mail/message if the person doesn't answer. Request for them to call you back. The reason for calling is to have a conversation! They will likely be delighted to receive a phone call that isn't a survey, sales call, or someone wanting something!

SOCIAL MEDIA

Use social media (Facebook, Twitter, etc.) when you want to publicly thank someone. This could be to thank a cookbook author for a great recipe, or to acknowledge the person in some way that will help promote their service or product.

Social media is great for a quick thank you. You can thank someone for dinner on Facebook and still follow up with a handwritten note.

When thanking on social media, the thank you may look like bragging, so choose your words carefully and determine if another method would be more appropriate. Don't use the thank you as a way to show off!

ONLINE SERVICES

There are two types of online services for writing thanking you notes. There are sites like *Postable.com*, where you can write the thank-you note while logged into their website. Then they print it and mail it for you. This type of service, usually offers an online address book where you can store the names and address of your contacts for free. Another benefit is that it removes the hassle of buying stamps.

If you still want a handwritten note, but don't want to write it yourself, there are services like *MailLift.com*. You provide them with the text, and then they will handwrite the note for you. This model may work best for businesses where the note can be from a team. Be aware: If the note is signed with your name, people may feel misled if they find out you didn't write the note yourself.

Q&A:
IF YOU MAKE A MISTAKE IN A HANDWRITTEN THANK-YOU NOTE, SHOULD YOU START OVER?

WHEN WRITING THANK-YOU NOTES, there may come a time when you spell a word wrong or want to change a word. With handwritten notes you have a choice to make: Should you start over or cross it out?

There is not an easy Yes or No answer for this question. It just depends on your situation and your personal preference. My mom always starts over, but I cross out in some situations.

A crossed out word may make the note feel more genuine. A crossed out word means the word was likely not copied from a template. Or maybe it was just spelled wrong. If you are paying $4.00 or more for a fancy high quality paper card, you also may not want to start over.

Start over when...

- **If you are writing the thank-you note after having a job interview.** The thank-you note could determine if you get another interview or the job. Make sure the thank-you note is not sloppy. No crossing out no matter how much you paid for the card!

- **The recipient is not someone you know well.** You want to make a good impression!

- **The person may put the thank-you note on display.** This could be if you are giving a thank-you note to a co-worker. Some of my co-workers display any note they are given. It's possible that other co-workers will read your note. Better to start over than to become known as the messy writer in your office.

- **You have several cross-outs in the same note.** One or two is okay, but if the thank-you note is only three sentences, then multiple mistakes may come across as sloppy and suggest you didn't care about what you were writing.

- **If you like everything to be neat**, then feel free to start over in any situation.

Leave it crossed out when...

- **The note is being sent to someone you know well.** I do this when writing thank-you notes to my parents, grandma, or siblings. We know each other well and have written enough thank-you notes to each other that a crossed out word is alright. They are likely not judging your penmanship.

- **It's your last thank-you note and it's not for a job interview.** If you don't have another blank card with which to start over, just keep going. Most people are forgiving and will be thrilled to be getting a thank-you note in the mail.

Q&A:
DO YOU SEND A THANK-YOU NOTE FOR A CARD?

PERHAPS, YOU HAVE RECEIVED a card for your birthday, congratulations, sympathy, a holiday, your wedding, or other occasion. Should you send a thank-you note for the card? The short answer is no. Sending a handwritten thank-you note in response to a card is not needed.

Acknowledging the card is thoughtful and often appreciated. This could be done in person or on the phone. Or a "Thank you for the card" text message, email, or social media message can be sent.

If you feel like you should (or if you just want to), go ahead and send a thank-you note for the card. Not sending a thank-you note for a card is only a general guideline. Remember, if you receive money in a card, you *do* need to thank the person for the money.

You might want to send a thank you for a card when...

- **You are touched or otherwise impressed by the card.** This could happen if you've received a birthday card for the first time as an adult. Perhaps your own immediate family does not send birthday cards. Then you get married or start dating someone. There may be people in the significant other's family that start sending you a birthday card each year. If you are moved by this, by all means, send a thank-you note card. This will let the sender know that the card was appreciated and made an impact.

- **You were surprised that you received the card from this particular person.** Perhaps it is a new friend or business contact. Send a card to keep the relationship going.

- **Someone sent you congratulations for a new job.** A follow up thank-you note could be used a networking opportunity.

- **Someone came to your wedding and gave you a card only—no other gift.** You could still thank them for coming to your wedding. Even if a gift was not in their budget, or they didn't give you a gift for some other reason, they still chose to spend their time at your wedding.

- **You want to!** If you really like sending cards, by all means send a thank you for the card. But do not expect a thank you for the thank-you note. It could turn into a never-ending cycle!

Another idea is to send a letter in return. You can mention the card in your letter, and then go on to write a letter that is longer than a typical thank-you note card.

Q&A:
WHAT SHOULD I DO WHEN I NEED TO WRITE LOTS OF THANK-YOU NOTES FOLLOWING AN EVENT?

EVENTS LIKE WEDDINGS AND GRADUATIONS tend to result in many gifts. When I got married, I felt a little overwhelmed by the amount of notes I had to write. Now that I'm older and looking back on this, I have thought about how I could have avoided the stress.

GET ORGANIZED.

I would have saved myself a lot of trouble if we had not written the names of the givers and the gifts on the back of an envelope. This led to not knowing who gave us the mini crock-pot and sending two thank-you notes for one gift!

Being organized before your event will help. Make a document that you can use to track the name of who gave each gift and what the gift was. You can do this in Excel or Word. Make a one-page grid and print it as many times as needed, or use lined notebook paper. Have columns for the date, the giver's name, gift, and thank-you note written. I have created a free downloadable template that you can use instead of creating your own. Simply go to *http://www.tonsofthanks.com/resources/* to get your copy. Fill out the first three columns as you open the gifts. And put a check mark in the last column as you write and mail the thank-you notes.

Take the notebook or the grid sheet with you to the event (say, a baby shower) or have it with you when opening your wedding or graduation gifts. Be diligent in using it! Write neatly. This will save you pain later.

If your event has already happened and you didn't write down who gave you what gift, do not panic. Write down as many gifts and the gift giver's name as possible. If you can't remember, still send a thank-you note. You will have to be a bit generic, and say, "Thank you for the gift," instead of referring to a specific item. This is better than not sending a thank-you note at all. Including another sentence thanking them for coming to the event will help it feel more real.

DO NOT WRITE ALL OF THE
THANK-YOU NOTES AT ONE TIME.

This is very important, so let me repeat: DO NOT write all the thank-you notes at one time. Also, do not feel like you need to write them all on the same day. Both will lead to that feeling of being overwhelmed and fatigue that we want to avoid. Plan to write the thank-you notes in several sessions.

Also, take breaks. I recommend writing no more than five notes at one time. If you have one-hundred notes to write and want to finish in a week, plan to write about fifteen a day. This can be done in about an hour and a half, if you spend no more than five minutes on each note and take a five-minute break after every five notes.

SHARE THE WORK.

If these notes are wedding thank-you notes, have your spouse help. The notes can be split between both of you. Staying organized will be important to ensure that you are not duplicating efforts and have not forgotten anyone.

SHIFT YOUR MINDSET.

Your mindset is important. If you think you will be overwhelmed, then you will feel overwhelmed. Decide that the thank-you note writing will be enjoyable. As you write each thank-you note, reflect on the gift and the giver and what they mean to you.

Remember how you felt when you opened the gift. Think about how you will enjoy the gift. Smile if they traveled a long way to attend your event.

THE EXAMPLES

Now that you have learned the "How" and the "Why" of writing thank-you notes, the remainder of the book will focus on situational examples. There are more than 400 examples from which to choose. The examples begin with general examples for gifts and money. Then the book is divided into sections: At the Office, Food, Holidays, Events, and People.

Some chapters will also include several tips to help you get started. You can read all the chapters at once to be prepared to write any type of thank-you note or skip around as the need arises.

Some examples are based on situations from my life. For example, in the after funeral chapter, one of the notes mentions grandma attending the same church for more than 100 years. My grandma attended the same church from the time she was born until she moved into a nursing home after her 100th birthday. Also, as of writing this, I have six cats that I love dearly, and therefore have included cat-themed examples throughout. Of course, "cat" can easily be substituted with any kind of pet in the examples.

MONEY AND GIFT CARDS

Money and gift cards are popular gifts for weddings, graduations, and birthdays. Also, sometimes money is given to help a person when they are in need. Anytime you receive money or a gift card, write a thank-you note to the person to show your gratitude and appreciation. The goal is to let the giver know how **their** money impacted your life, even if it was something fun or frivolous.

The two most common scenarios that unfold when money is received as a gift are spending the money and saving the money. When writing the note, include how you will spend the money or for what you will be saving it.

Tips:

- Include what you will be doing or did with the money.

- **Mention the occasion.** If the money/gift card was given for a specific occasion, such as a birthday or anniversary, the occasion can be included in the card. For example, "birthday money."

- **Do not mention the amount that was given.** The person will know how much they gave to you.

- **Don't forget checks!** If the cash was in the form of a check, it is okay to say, "Thank you for the check." Also, checks should be acknowledged promptly as the sender will be wondering if their check made it to you.

- **Instead of saying "money," it is okay to say "gift."**

- **For gift cards, mention the name of the store or restaurant.**

- **Don't make things up.** If you really do not know how you will spend the money or what you are saving for, it is okay to say that too. Say, "I will be adding this money to my savings until I have a need for it."

- **Be honest.** Don't say, "I am saving the money for college," if that isn't true.

- **Include at least two sentences.** Only saying "Thanks for the money!" may leave the giver wondering what you did with it.

- If applicable, let the giver know how their money helped you.

Examples:

I appreciate the check you mailed. The timing was perfect as I was not going to be able to pay the full gas bill. Your money will keep my heat on. God bless!

Thank you for the birthday money. I had fun spending it on Amazon. I ordered a new cookbook and a few other books that have been on my want list, including [Book Title]. *I am looking forward to hours of enjoyable reading.*

I was very surprised to receive your card and gift in the mail today. I used it to splurge on dinner at my favorite sushi restaurant. I felt happy to be able to sit at the sushi bar and be able to order anything I wanted. Thank you very much!

Thank you for the gift card to [Store Name]. *I love shopping there. I picked out some new wool socks to keep me warm this winter.*

Thank you for the graduation gift. I plan to save the money for future college-related expenses. I also enjoyed visiting with you at my graduation party.

I loved the gift card to [Store Name]*! I am saving them up towards* [Expensive Item]. *I should have enough saved up by this time next year.*

We are thankful for the anniversary money. We are currently building our emergency fund and will be adding your generous gift to the fund. We are looking forward to the day when minor "emergencies" feel like an inconvenience instead of an emergency as we will have the money in the bank to cover it.

We love eating at [Restaurant Name]*! Thank you very much for the gift card. We will be eating there very soon and will enjoy being able to order anything we want from the menu, including dessert!*

The gift card to [Store Name] *is awesome! I was very surprised and the timing is perfect as we found out that* [Spouse's Name] *will be laid off for the next two weeks. We will use the gift card on groceries and pet food.*

Thank you for sending the cash. I was able to use it right away to fill up the gas tank in my car. I very much enjoyed having you pay for the gas. I will also be able to get a new shirt to wear to the office.

I was surprised when the stray cats showed up in the back yard. I was more surprised when your gift card to [Store Name] *arrived in the mail. I will be using it to get more food for the cats while I search for homes for them. Thank you for helping support these cats!*

Sending me cash for my birthday was very thoughtful of you. I look forward to spending it on [What You Plan to Buy]. *Thank you for being so generous!*

I was excited to get a card from you for my graduation. The cash was a wonderful surprise. [Spouse's Name] *and I will use it towards a fancy dinner when we go out to celebrate.*

Thank you for the check for our wedding. We are saving it towards a down payment on a new house. We hope to have enough saved within the next year. Your check will help us reach that goal a bit sooner than planned.

DONATIONS

WHATEVER YOUR CAUSE MAY BE, getting donations can be a challenge. If you received a donation, be sure to follow up with a thank-you note. Showing appreciation will build good will with the donor and perhaps lead to more donations in the future.

Tips:

- **Show the impact.** If it makes sense for your situation, include a sentence about how you/your cause are benefiting from the donation. There are many, many things that can be donated: cars, money for various causes, cat surgery, scholarship money, medical expenses, etc. With sites like Go Fund Me, the possibilities have become endless.

- **Write more.** If a donation was made directly to you (not to an organization), you may want to opt for a full-length letter to express your gratitude and show how much the donation means to your life. You can explain your background and how you expect the donation will change your life.

Examples:

Thank you for donating to help cover the cost of my cat's unexpected surgery. [Cat's Name] *feels like part of the family. I am happy to report that she did very well and the tumor has been removed. She is expected to make a full recovery!*

We are very grateful for your contribution to the [Description/Name] *Scholarship fund. This scholarship is awarded to students that meet our criteria for* [Goal of Scholarship]. *Your generous donation will help two students with their first year of college tuition.*

I am grateful to receive your old car! I was in a bind when the transmission dropped out of my car. I will be able to get to and from work now. As you know, I am struggling to make ends meet, and this car is a true blessing.

I appreciate the financial donation you've made to my political campaign. Your contribution will help us reach more potential voters. I am grateful for your support.

Thank you for helping me with my mounting medical expenses. The recovery from the accident has been long and expensive. Because of your donation, I should be able to have all the bills paid by the end of this year!

This year has been interesting! The dogs I rescued are recovering and finally putting on some weight. Thank you for providing the dog food for them. I hope to be able to find quality homes for them soon.

We were surprised when Aunt [Name] *passed away unexpectedly. She was a lovely lady and unfortunately she was living paycheck to paycheck. We are grateful that you were able to cover the funeral expenses.*

My sisters and I are thankful for your support during the various fundraisers for our church mission trip. The small donations for Wednesday night dinners at church add up to a lot over the months. And we thank you for the check you mailed. The mission trip was wonderful and we will tell you all about it the next time we see you.

Thank you for donating your leftover paint to our center. We were able to give every room a fresh coat. The kids are enjoying the bright colors! We appreciate you that you thought of us!

I feel very blessed by your generosity. Paying my first and last month's rent at the new apartment was very kind of you. I am excited to be close enough to walk to my job and will be working on paying off my debts and building savings. Thank you for helping me to get this apartment without incurring more debt.

AT
THE
OFFICE

AT THE OFFICE INTRODUCTION

MANY PEOPLE SPEND more (non-sleeping) hours at work each day than they do at home. This makes for plenty of opportunities to thank those around you in the workplace. People, including your co-workers, like to be recognized for their efforts!

My commute to the office is about an hour long. One day I had a hair appointment scheduled in the same city where I work but realized I had forgotten my purse at home! Given the long drive-time, going home to retrieve it was not a good option; I also didn't want to take a half day of vacation to be able to go home and get back in time for the appointment. I decided to ask a co-worker for a one-day loan for the cost of the appointment. She said yes!

She didn't have the cash on her and had to find an ATM during lunch. She was happy to help me out even though it was an inconvenience to her. I wrote her a handwritten note to thank her for helping me out in my time of need and placed the cash I owed her inside the card.

Another time I wrote a thank-you note at work was when I needed help with a project. I reached out for help and this particular person's involvement was more than what was expected. She also did excellent work and helped that phase of the project go smoothly. When it was finished I wrote her a thank-you note.

I also relied on a co-worker for helping figuring out issues with another project. He stepped in, helped me find the problem, explained the part of the process where I had gone wrong, and smoothed things over with the recipient. I was very thankful that he helped, as he saved me hours and hours of time. He also received a handwritten thank-you note.

The response I have received from co-workers has varied. Some still have not acknowledged the note (which is okay). Others have thanked me for the note and have them on display at their desk. Regardless of the response you may receive, I encourage you to send a thank-you note to someone in your workplace at every opportunity.

I hope these stories have given you some inspiration to thank your co-workers! Examples can be found on the following pages.

THANKING YOUR BOSS FOR A RAISE AND/OR BONUS

WE MAY FEEL LIKE we should be getting paid more for all the hard work we've done but it is not guaranteed. Unless getting a raise or bonus is written into the terms of your employment, you are not automatically entitled to get a raise. Remember that our salaries are the amount we agree to work for when we choose to work for a company or individual.

Saying thank you shows your gratitude for what you've been given. Even if your raise or bonus was less that you expected (we always want more, right?), we should still say thank you. It could have been nothing!

One of the easiest ways to thank your boss is with a handwritten thank-you note. Email is easier and faster. However, a handwritten note will have a greater impact. They take a bit more time and feel more personal. I have not seen a boss (or any co-worker) print an email thank-you and display it on their desk or somewhere in their cube. But I have seen many handwritten cards on display.

Tips:

- **Be mindful of what you say**, as you don't know who else will see the note. Even if you decide to send an email, someone else could still see it.

- **Do not include the amount of your raise or bonus in the thank-you note.** It is possible that not everyone on your team received the same percentage or amount. This will help avoid any potential drama if someone else happens to read the card.

- **Be discreet.** In most cases when you receive money, I recommend telling the giver what you will be doing with the money. *This situation does not qualify.* Your boss does not need to know how you are spending your money.

- **Don't complain.** If you are feeling bitter about the amount you received, wait a few days to write the note. Better to wait than to regret words written in haste!

- **Don't be a kiss-up.** This is not the time to suck up by telling your boss how great he/she is. A little bit is okay, but don't go overboard!

- **Use a simple note card design.** Do not let choosing the design be an obstacle to writing the thank-you note. If you really can't decide, send it in an email.

- **Don't forget the holidays.** If you receive a bonus shortly before Christmas or year-end, you can also wish your boss a Merry Christmas (or happy holidays if you are not sure if they celebrate Christmas) and Happy New Year.

- **Think ink.** I like to write my thank-you note to my boss using purple ink, as my love for purple is quite well known at my office. You may want to stick to a traditional blue or black. Don't use a cheap pen that leaves behind ink globs. No one wants to see ink globs. Ever.

- **Go the distance.** If your boss is in a different location than you, you can still mail a thank-you note. The address for their location should be available in an internal directory (or you can ask them).

Examples:

I want to thank you for this year's raise. It's always nice to be appreciated financially!

I've enjoyed working with you this year and have learned a lot from you. Thank you for the raise. I really appreciate it. Getting a bonus is awesome too!

Thank you for the raise and bonus. I am thrilled that we met our targets to receive both this year! I hope next year is even better for the company.

I am excited to have received a bonus. The timing is perfect, just before Christmas. I hope you have a nice holiday vacation. See you next year!

Thank you for the raise. I also appreciate the time you spent helping me with [Issue] *this year. I am thankful for what I learned.*

I am glad to be on your team. Thank you for the annual merit increase. A little more in the pocket is always appreciated!

Being recognized with a raise and a bonus feels great! Thank you for the financial appreciation.

Thank you for the bonus! It was very unexpected. I greatly appreciate it and I'm thankful that our team met the financial goals this quarter.

What a treat! Thank you for including me in the bonus distribution this quarter. I was very surprised since I started a few days late to be officially eligible. The bonus is much appreciated.

Thank you for the raise and bonus. I look forward to another successful year with [Company Name]. *I also appreciate how much individual training you've given me in the past six months. I understand the position and tasks much better now.*

GIFTS, HELP, AND ACTS OF KINDNESS

THERE ARE MANY TIMES when we receive a gift or some form of help. Sometimes, we benefit from a random act of kindness. Let's say, you've noticed someone helping out with your special needs child and want to thank him or her. Perhaps someone did something nice for you while you were out of town. Maybe you noticed someone doing something beneficial for the community, workplace, or church. The list could go on and on! The examples in this chapter will focus on the random unexpected gifts, help, or act of kindness that make a difference in the lives of others.

Tips:

- **Refer directly to the gift.** In any situation, be sure to mention what you are thanking the giver for specifically.

- **Honor the occasion.** If the gift/help was given for a specific reason or occasion, such as a birthday, anniversary, or emergency, say so. For example, "birthday gift."

- **Tell them what happened next.** It is nice to mention how the gift, help, or act of kindness impacted your life. This will make the giver feel appreciated.

EXAMPLES:

Gifts

Thank you for the [Gift]. *I love it! I am feeling loved since you thought of me while you were on vacation with your family. I will enjoy the* [Gift] *often.*

My cats love the gourmet cat treats that you picked up for them. Thinking of them when you were getting stuff for your dog was very thoughtful. Thank you for your generosity!

Help

I noticed how much time you spend helping [Child's Name]. *I appreciate your kindness and patience with him. You've gained his trust and he does better in class when you are there. Thank you for your efforts.*

Thank you for helping with [Child's Name]*'s math homework. I could show him the way I was taught, but he will get marked down if he doesn't do it using the Common Core method. I am grateful that you were able to explain it to him in a way that made sense.*

I am thankful for your tutoring program. We didn't know how to help [Child's Name] *and heard about your program. He's doing so much better with his schoolwork now. Your program has changed his life for the better!*

We are grateful for you for retrieving our mail each day while we were on vacation. With the post office so far away, it is much faster to get our mail from you when we return. Thank you for being a trusted neighbor!

What a wonderful friend you are! I appreciate that I can count on you to be there when I need help. Can you believe that I ran out of gas again? Thank you for coming to my rescue. I really need to get that gas gauge replaced soon.

Acts of Kindness

I was super surprised that you mowed my lawn last week. When I asked you to keep an eye on my house while I was away, I didn't expect you to do yard work for me. I am very happy and thankful that I came home to a lawn that looked fabulous.

I've noticed how kind you are to the children at church. I appreciate how you always take the time to answer their questions. My [Son/Daughter], [Child's Name], looks forward to seeing you every Sunday. Your attention makes [His/Her] day.

Thank you for spending some time with me when I found out that my grandma passed away. Receiving the news while I was at work was difficult. I appreciate your friendship and covering for me during that meeting so I can have some privacy to process her passing. She would have liked you!

THANKING THE BOSS FOR LUNCH

THERE ARE THREE EXCEPTIONS to thanking your boss with a thank-you note for lunch:

1. If the boss is having lunch with you to fire you or lay you off, then a thank-you note is not recommended.

2. The boss is also a close friend and you go out often together. This would fall under the casual lunch situation, which doesn't need a thank-you note.

3. If the lunch was a working lunch rather than the boss taking you out, a thank-you note is not needed.

Of course, if you still want to write a thank-you note, you absolutely can!

Tips:

*   **Professionalism first!** Asking the boss for his home address is not professional. Write the thank-you note and then hand it to him. Also, you may leave it on his desk. If your business/office has a mailbox system, leave it in his mailbox.

- **Find a nice design.** When choosing the design, pick a theme that you know your boss will like. Or go with a simple classic thank you card that just says "Thank You" or "Thanks" on the front.

- **Write the note using a pen, as pencil will fade over time.**

- **Don't be generic.** Thank the boss for the specific reason they had lunch with you and also for their time. If they shared something personal, you could mention that as well.

- **Be prompt.** Send the note within a few days of having lunch together.

Template:

Dear [Insert boss's name],

Thank you for taking me out to lunch at [Insert restaurant name]. *I enjoyed our visit and learning about your family. I appreciate the time you took out of your day. I enjoyed learning more about* [Insert project name]. *I am looking forward to working on it with you.*

Thanks Again,

[Sign your name]

EXAMPLES:

One-on-One Lunch

Thank you for taking me out to lunch. I enjoyed visiting with you. As you know, [Restaurant Name] *is my favorite. I know it is not your favorite, so I appreciate you taking me there even more!*

I enjoyed our lunch last week. I appreciate that you took time out of your day to have lunch with me. I liked learning about [Project Name] *that is coming up and am thankful for the advance notice.*

Thanks so much for lunch. I feel recognized and appreciated for my portion of the work on [Project Name]. *I am looking forward to being the leader of the next project.*

Having lunch with you outside of the office was awesome. Thank you for taking me out! I enjoyed hearing more about your family, especially how the kids keep you busy with hockey.

Thanks for lunch yesterday! It was an unexpected and welcome surprise. I was having a terrible day and lunch out cheered me up. I'm glad I can count on you to be a good friend when I need one.

The lunch with you and learning more about [Client Name] *was enlightening. I feel more informed about their needs, which will help me support them better. Thanks for the meal too!*

Thank you for taking me out for lunch for Administrative Assistant's day! I feel appreciated and grateful for having you as my boss. I'm glad you were able to fit me into your schedule.

Thank you for lunch yesterday. I liked getting to know you a bit better outside the office. The stories you shared about your family were funny. It sounds like you have a great relationship with your children.

The stories you shared at lunch yesterday were amazing. You've had quite an interesting life leading up to working at [Company Name]. *I was impressed with how you overcame [Challenge]. Thank you for taking me to lunch and sharing so much about your background. I am grateful to have you as my boss.*

Lunch was wonderful yesterday! Thank you for taking me out to celebrate my promotion. I am happy to be on your team and appreciate both lunch and the promotion. I also enjoyed our conversation and learning about your kids.

Thanks for picking up the tab at lunch on [Day of the Week]. That was a pleasant surprise. We should go to lunch more often. I didn't realize we shared the same passion for [Shared Interest]. I could talk about [Shared Interest] for hours! It was also nice to talk about something other than work projects.

Last week's lunch was fantastic—I am thrilled with the promotion. Thank you for taking me out and surprising me. It feels good to be recognized and I look forward to my new responsibilities.

I am happy that I won the contest to have lunch with you. Thanks for letting me choose the restaurant. I enjoyed the time outside of the office. Thank you for sharing your wisdom on how to succeed in this position.

I was very excited to learn that you have two rescue cats at lunch this week. Thank you for taking me out and talking about non-work stuff for a bit. I had a nice time visiting with you and hope we can do it again sometime soon.

Thank you for lunch. I was very pleased to learn more about [Project Name] and that you have selected me to be the lead on it. I am very excited about this opportunity. I enjoy working on your team.

I enjoyed discussing [Book Title] *with you over lunch yesterday. Hearing your views on* [Book Subject] *was interesting as they were not things I had considered. Thanks again for lunch!*

Lunch was great last week! I was surprised by how much we had in common. I could talk about [Shared Interest] *all day! I enjoyed the food too. Thanks for taking me out.*

I'm glad you decided to take each team member out to lunch with you. Team lunches are great but sometimes we only are able to talk to whoever is seated next to us. I enjoyed hearing more about your background and [Story Your Boss Shared]. *Thanks for the lunch.*

Team Lunch

Thanks for taking the group out to lunch. Spending time together outside of the office helps us to bond as a team. It was a nice opportunity to get to know the newer people better.

Wow! Lunch at [Restaurant Name] *was great. It feels awesome to work at a place that has the budget for expensive meals. And the dessert was awesome too. This is a great team! I'm so proud of what this team has been able to accomplish.*

I had a great time at [Restaurant Name] *with the team. Thank you for taking us out. It is a nice memory for our team and helped us get to know each other better.*

The team lunch this week was amazing. Thank you for taking us out and getting to know us better and giving us a chance to get to know you. I was happy to learn that your family has two [Pet]*!*

I really like this team! I look forward to the weekly team lunch every week. Thanks for ordering in from [Restaurant Name] *this week. It really hit the spot and I like trying new food.*

Our conversation was very thought provoking and should help us improve our productivity. Thank you for arranging the private room at [Restaurant Name] *as it allowed us to easily hear what everyone one was saying.*

Celebrating the promotions on the team last week was fun. I like being on a team that recognizes accomplishments! Thanks for taking all of us out. Hopefully, we will have a reason to do it again soon.

Lunch was awesome yesterday! The food and time spent with the team were both amazing. I enjoyed interacting with you and the others. Thank you!

My stomach is still sore from laughing so much at lunch yesterday. Thank you for uniting the team with your humorous stories. This was a lunch we will never forget.

I was very surprised that you took us to [Restaurant Name] *for lunch. The environment made it feel like more than just another team lunch. Thank you for recognizing our efforts on making the sales deal with* [Client].

Thanks for the welcome lunch at [Restaurant Name]. *I had a nice time and enjoyed getting to know the rest of the team better. I was able to connect with* [Coworker Name] *as we watch some of the same TV programs. I feel like I made a friend because of the lunch as so far we've been too busy to socialize much in the office.*

The team lunch was fun yesterday. I am thankful that we were all able to make it and that went to [Restaurant Name] *which is one of my favorite restaurants. I appreciate the company picking up the tab too! It feels good to be recognized for our hard work.*

I enjoyed bonding with the team. I liked getting to know each other better by hearing everyone's answers to your atypical icebreaker questions. You are very creative! Thanks again for lunch!

Thank you for the team lunch. Discussing [Book Title] *with the team at lunch was a wonderful idea. I got more out of the book by hearing what others have learned from it.*

I enjoyed the team lunch last week. Asking everyone to share his or her most memorable moment while working on [Project] *was fun and gave us a chance to hear from everyone. Thank you for treating us to lunch at* [Restaurant Name].

Having a team lunch on the picnic tables was a creative way to have a team lunch with no cost to the company. Thank you for organizing it and encouraging everyone to bring their own lunch from home. The variety of lunch items was amazing and gave us a lot to talk about other than work. It turns out I am not the only food snob in the group!

Thank you for the two-hour team lunch! I am glad you arranged it when the whole team could go and no one needed to feel rushed. The lunch helped to build my camaraderie with the others. I was excited to learn that [Coworker Name] *volunteers at the humane society.*

I had a great time at the team lunch. Thanks for treating us to [Restaurant Name]. *Getting away from the office was a nice break. Time well spent on team bonding.*

Thanks for the team lunch on [Day of the Week]. *I really enjoyed the* [Dish Name]. *It was delicious! I am grateful to have been introduced to* [Restaurant Name] *and spending time with the team was nice too.*

Food can bring people together like nothing else. Thank you for taking the team out. I had a nice time visiting with other team members and look forward to the next team lunch.

THANKING YOUR COWORKERS

Coworkers. They can help you, give you gifts, or take you to lunch.

If you are working a full-time job away from home, you may be spending more time with your coworkers than your family. Take a few moments to let them know they are appreciated.

There are general examples below for when they help you or do something nice. Then there are also sections for wedding and baby gifts that come from coworkers.

Tips:

- **Don't type it. . .**If you are thanking one coworker, I recommend a handwritten note. Most people love to display them on their desks!

- **. . .Unless you're sending it a group.** If you are thanking a group of co-workers, I recommend sending one email to everyone.

- **Spread the news.** Another way to thank them is to let the boss know what they did for you! An easy way to do this when sending a thank-you email is to copy the boss on the email.

Examples:

> *Thank you for covering my work while I was out. I was glad to be able to turn over* [Project Name] *to you without having to worry about it. I see you did an excellent job handling the details. The client is pleased!*

> *I appreciate your help with figuring out the problem with my logic in the custom programming. I was stumped and your solution was perfect. I am thankful that I can rely on you as a resource.*

> *Thank you for taking me to lunch! That was an unexpected surprise. I enjoyed visiting with you and learning more about your kids. Also,* [Restaurant Name] *is one of my favorites!*

> *The magnet you give me is awesome. I love that it is* [Your Favorite Color] *and also functional. You know how I feel about clutter! The magnet is also powerful enough to held up the report that I reference nearly every day.*

> *Thanks for bringing in treats for the team every Friday! Your baked goods are delicious, and I look forward to them every week. They are the best part of Friday!*

> *Once again, you were there to help me out. Thanks for being dependable and also having the knowledge to solve the programming problems. I have learned a lot from you.*

> *Thank you for helping me last week. I was totally lost in the weeds. Your second set of eyes quickly found the issue. I was very happy to have the problem solved!*

THANKING YOUR COWORKERS
FOR WEDDING GIFTS

Thank you, team, for the wedding gifts. The shower was a nice surprise. The kitchen utensils are wonderful and will be helpful once we are married and cooking our own food. We've been spoiled by our mothers!

The gifts you chose for us are perfect. We will enjoy the [Gifted Items]. *We appreciate your generosity as we start our life together!*

My husband and I thank you for the wedding money. We will use it towards a dining room table set. We hope to see you all at the wedding!

Thank you for the food processor and blender set. I am excited to use them for food prep and making dressing. It was very nice of you all to contribute towards gifts for us!

We thank you for the wedding shower and gifts. The cake was great and we love the flannel sheets. Also, thank you to all of you for covering my work while we are on the honeymoon!

THANKING YOUR COWORKERS FOR BABY GIFTS

I am excited to try out cloth diapers when the baby comes. I had no idea there were so many different brands. Thank you for providing a wide selection. I will try them all to see which brand baby and I like best.

Thank you for the Pack and Play. This will be wonderful to have when we visit family. I'm happy to work on such a generous team! The little toys are cute too!

The outfits for the twins are adorable! I love the colors and that you found cute stuff for [Boy/Girl] *twins. Thank you so much!*

Thank you for the baby gifts. The toys are interactive which seems like a good thing these days. Thank you for your support as my husband and I begin a new chapter in life with our first baby!

Wow! Thanks for the stroller. I plan to walk every day once the baby comes. Is that realistic? We can have baby chats once I return to work! Thanks again!

JOB INTERVIEW

A THANK-YOU NOTE FOLLOWING an interview is a great way to make another connection with the interviewer. In addition to thanking them for their time, you can remind them of your skills or include something you forgot to mention during the interview.

Tips:

- **Mailing a handwritten thank-you note may make you stand out.** According to Forbes,[1] it depends on the industry, as some would prefer an email thank-you.

- **Time is of the essence.** If you have no confidence that a handwritten note would actually reach your interviewer in a timely manner, then email the thank-you note. If you know someone already working there, ask them how mail is handled to learn if emailing or mailing the thank-you would be better.

---

1   Tiffin, M. (2014, June 9). Interview Etiquette: Is The Handwritten Thank You Note Outdated? Retrieved April 02, 2016, from *http://www.forbes.com/sites/learnvest/2014/06/09/interview-etiquette-is-the-handwritten-thank-you-note-outdated/3/*

- **Act fast.** If you are interviewing for a job that is not local, it may be better to email the thank-you note. The goal is to have the thank-you note arrive before the second round of interviews or hiring decisions are made. Sometimes, this will not be possible even when mailing the thank-you note the same day as the interview.

- **Don't write an essay.** A handwritten note will need to be shorter to fit on the card. An email can be longer, but bear in mind that if it's too long, the interviewer may not read it!

- **You can type it out.** Another option is to write your letter in a word processing program and then print it and mail it. If you choose this option, be sure to sign your name using a pen on the printed letter.

Also, please keep in mind that while thank-you notes are a nice gesture and another contact point, they may not have any impact on whether you are offered the job or make it to the next round of interviewing. Some interviewers may not care either way. Others may disqualify you for NOT sending a thank-you. The result is not something that can easily be predicted.

POST INTERVIEW THANK-YOU NOTE DOS AND DON'TS:

- **DON'T** send a thank-you email from the parking lot immediately after the interview. Wait at least a few hours or until the next morning.

- **DON'T** use "Mrs." if you are not sure if the woman who interviewed you is married. Stick with "Ms."

- **DON'T** say anything untrue. You want to look as good as possible, but lies may come back to haunt you later.

- **DON'T** mention salary or money.

- **DO** thank everyone that interviewed you. If someone didn't ask questions, you could still thank them for their time.

- **DO** send handwritten notes within a day of the interview (when mailing).

- **DO** include the title of the position for which you interviewed. It's possible that the interviewer is interviewing for other positions concurrently. You want to be sure they connect the thank-you note to you and your interview.

- **DO** mention a topic from the interview. This will help them connect the note to you as they could be interviewing many other candidates.

- **DO** send a thank-you note even if you are no longer interested in the position. You can still thank the interviewer for their time and explaining the position.

- **DO** include a specific date and time when you will call them to follow up in the note when thanking your main contact.

- **DO** double-check your spelling and grammar. If sending a handwritten note, you can write it out in a program with spell check and then copy it to your note card.

- **DO** start over if you make a mistake in a handwritten note.

- **DO** use paragraphs. Large blocks of text with five or more sentences are harder to read. Some people will not read your note if it is one giant paragraph.

Template:

Knowing what to say in a post-interview thank-you note can be a challenge. The following template and examples will help you get started. What you choose to say is dependent on the position and context of conversation.

Thank-you notes for job interviews will usually be longer than those written for a gift. And will also have more than one paragraph. Since these examples contain more content, I've included the opening and closing instead of only the meat of the thank-you note.

Dear [Insert interviewer name],

Thank you for interviewing me on [Insert day of interview] *for* [Insert position/job title]. *I appreciate the opportunity and your interest in me.*

[Sentence mentioning something from the interview]. [Sentence iterating your interest and skills].

[Say when you will follow up with a call to check on the status of job].

Sincerely,

[Sign your name]

EXAMPLES:

Example #1

Dear [Interviewer Name],

Thank you for meeting with me on [Day of Interview] *to discuss* [Position/Job Title]. *I appreciate your time and thorough explanation of the role.*

I feel that my skills in the game design will allow me to bring value to the game development time. I have over five years of experience with [Software the Company Uses]. *I was happy to hear that you are also a Tetris fan!*

I also have spent time using [Software Not Mentioned in Interview] *and can share my knowledge with the team.*

I will call you at 10:00 on Monday to check on the status of the position.

Sincerely,

[Your Name]

Example #2

Dear [Interviewer Name],

Thank you for meeting with me on Tuesday to discuss [Position/Job Title]. *I am thankful for the opportunity and the time you spent explaining the position in detail.*

After learning more about it, I am very interested in joining your team. My past work with problem solving will make me an asset to [Company Name]. *I found your "what would you do" scenarios intriguing!*

I will plan to follow up with you at 10:00 on Monday to check on the status of the position.

Sincerely,

[Your Name]

Example #3 — *This example is for a note to the interviewer in a group interview that didn't ask you many (if any) questions and is not your main follow up contact:*

Dear [Interviewer Name],

I enjoyed meeting with you last Tuesday about [Position/Job Title] *in your department. I appreciate that you took time out of your day to meet with me.*

It was a pleasure meeting you and learning more about the position. I would enjoy working on your team.

Sincerely,

[Your Name]

Example #4

Dear [Interviewer Name],

I appreciate the time you set aside to meet with me on Tuesday to discuss [Position/Job Title]. *I am excited about the position after learning more about it.*

I was surprised to learn that we both know [Name]! *As I mentioned in the interview* [He/She] *is the reason I became interested in* [Work Related to Position].

My skills with [Program Relevant to Position] *would allow me to quickly contribute to the success of the projects on your team. I also enjoy learning new programs and will commit to learning* [New Program] *as soon as possible.*

I will follow up with you at [Time of Day] *on* [Day of Week] *regarding this position.*

Sincerely,

[Your Name]

Example #5

Dear [Interviewer Name],

I am grateful for our discussion last week on [Day of the Week] *about* [Position/Job Title]. *After learning more about the requirements, I am confident that I would excel in the position.*

As we discussed during the interview, I have [Number] *years of experience with* [Program]. *I enjoy showing others the lesser-known features of* [Program] *as they can improve productivity and make the program easier to use.*

I was excited to hear your plan for expanding the team and increasing the number of programs used. I have used many programs, such as [Program Names]. *I tend to keep up with the latest programs and learn them quickly.*

I will call you next week at [Time of Day] *on* [Day of the Week] *to follow up on the status of this position.*

Best Regards,

[Your Name]

Example #6

Dear [Interviewer Name],

I was very excited to meet you last [Day of the Week] *about* [Position/Job Title]. *I've been interested in working for* [Company Name] *since I read in* [News

Source] *that they are debt free. Avoiding debt aligns with my personal values.*

After learning more about [Position], *I feel that it would be a great fit. I enjoy working with others in a team environment and have spent the last* [Number] *of years working on marketing projects. With the skills I have in* [Program Name] *I would fit in well with your team.*

Also, I want to let you know that I've worked with [Employee Name] *in that past at* [Previous Employer]. *We were in the communications department and worked on several projects together.*

I will contact you next week at [Time of Day] *on* [Day of the Week] *to follow up regarding the status of this position.*

Regards,

[Your Name]

Example #7 — Declining the position

[Interviewer Name],

Thank you for taking the time to interview me for [Position]. *I appreciate the time you took out of your day to go over it with me. After learning more about the position, I am no longer interested in pursuing this opportunity. I feel like I would not be a good fit based on the details you shared.*

[Company Name] *sounds like a great company. If other positions open up that are related to* [Area of Interest], *I will reapply.*

I enjoyed meeting you and learning more about
[Company Name] *and hope that our paths may cross
again in the future.*

Sincerely,

[Your Name]

Example #8

[Interviewer Name],

I am grateful for the time we spent together on [Day
of the Week] *discussing* [Position]. *As I shared in the
interview, I feel that that position would be a great fit
due to my experience with* [Required Skill].

I was also excited to learn that [Company Name] *is on
the leading edge of technology and uses the latest versions
of all programs. I believe this helps to keep* [Company
Name] *ahead of the competition. The team environment
sounds conducive to solving issues as I like to talk
through my ideas with others.*

*I also enjoyed hearing the stories about your cats learning
to get along. As mentioned, I've rescued a few from my
backyard and can relate to the challenges.*

I will follow up next week at [Time of Day] *on* [Day of
the Week] *by phone regarding the status of this position.*

Kind Regards,

[Your Name]

Example #9

[Interviewer Name],

Thank you for discussing [Position] *with me on* [Day of the Interview]. *Now that I've had time to reflect on the interview, I continue to be excited about the position.*

I feel that I would fit in at [Company Name] *with my writing abilities. As I mentioned in the interview, I've written hundreds of articles as a freelancer about* [Topic]. *I would enjoy sharing my knowledge about* [Topic] *with members of your team.*

I appreciate that you shared that you have also spent time in [Branch of Armed Forces]. *I learned the value of discipline and hard work while serving.*

I will follow up at [Time of Day] *on* [Day of the Week] *by phone regarding the status of this position. Meanwhile, feel free to contact me if you have any further questions.*

Sincerely,

[Your Name]

Example #10 — To thank someone you had contact with, but did not interview you (ex. recruiter, administrative assistant).

Dear [Name],

Thank you for your efforts in organizing my interview for [Position] *with* [Primary Interview Contact]. *I appreciate how quickly you returned my emails regarding the interview time and for help with directions once inside the building.*

Sincerely,

[Your Name]

THANK THE BOSS
ON BOSS'S DAY

Boss's Day is on October 16th in the United States, unless it falls on a weekend. Some people give gifts on Boss's day, but here we will focus on the gift of your words expressed in a thank-you note! Handwritten notes may help you stand out— you can even send a gift *and* a thank-you note, if you'd like!

You Can Thank Your Boss For...

- Their support throughout the year

- Their support recently

- Training

- Mentoring

- Lunch (read the chapter *Thanking The Boss For Lunch*)

- To express gratitude for a raise or bonus read chapter *Thanking Your Boss For A Raise And/Or Bonus.*

- Flexibility

- Being an awesome caring boss

- Whatever you'd like that is appropriate for your boss.

Tips:

- **Do not include anything confidential** as others may see your note (even if it is in an email).

- **Don't compare your boss to another supervisor or higher-up.** That is a little tacky.

- **Get creative if you have to.** If you don't have a good boss (or if you don't like your boss), try to find one thing that you can thank them for. If you can't come up with anything, don't write a note—and consider looking for another job!

- **Don't overthink it.** The note can start with "Happy Boss's Day!" and end with "Have a great day!" Just sandwich your reason for thanking your boss in between the two.

- Compliments are also nice!

Examples:

Thank you for providing so much support recently on [Project Name]. *Learning the different roles of the project has been a challenge for me. I am grateful that you were willing to spend extra time with me explaining the details.*

I am very thankful that you have arranged work from home days for me. This has made appointments for my cats and doctor's appointments much easier to get to. And I've been able to have breakfast with my husband more often as well.

I appreciate that you are not only my boss but also my friend. Thank you for asking about my family and for covering work for me while I had dental appointments. This has been a trying year for me and I'm grateful that I didn't need to worry about time off of work being a problem.

Thank you for sending me to the training for [Subject]. This has changed that way I work on [Process]. I am happy that you encouraged me to go!

This last year has been interesting! Thank you for helping me along the way as I learned new customers. Your support made it much easier and I'm glad I can always come to you with questions!

I love working for you! Your mentoring on how to become a leader has changed my outlook on the business world. I am excited to learn more and more from you. Let's do lunch again soon!

Thank you for being understanding when I misunderstood the policy for taking time off at the last minute. I am glad that I was able to keep my job! What a relief as I enjoy working for [Company Name].

The recent training you did on [Topic] was fantastic. I look forward to learning more from you and continuing to improve my skills. I also appreciate the team lunches we've had this year.

You are a wonderful boss! I am happy that I was assigned to your team as I have learned a lot from you. I am amazed at how you are able to explain problems in a way that I can quickly understand.

I am grateful for all of you support. Working with [Client Name] has been a challenge for me and I'm thankful that you have been able to be on the calls. Your communication skills are starting to rub off on me!

THANK YOUR EMPLOYEES

IF YOU ARE A BOSS, I encourage you to thank your employees often. You could send them an appreciation message via email or write them a handwritten note. Thank them for their hard work, good customer service, excellent performance, and years of service.

National Employee Appreciation Day is celebrated the first Friday in March in the United States and Canada. While I recommend thanking your employees year round, do not neglect to thank them on National Employee Appreciation Day.

I have been an employee for over twenty years. As an employee, I can say that being thanked and appreciated feels good. I also have a better impression of the bosses I've had that said "thank you" on a regular basis. Some bosses may feel that employee's salary is a thank you. Salary is expected in exchange for doing the job. Money isn't everything. Saying thank you shows appreciation for the work that is being done.

Tips:

- **Be specific.** If you say, "You are great, Thanks for all you do," it's too generic to be meaningful. Your employee may wonder if you know how they spend their time.

- **Thank-you emails** can also be sent out to the entire team. And it's also nice when the boss brings in breakfast (bagels, donuts, or healthy breakfast foods) to the office on the day he/she is thanking the team.

- **You have options.** When thanking one person, I recommend a handwritten thank-you note. Almost anything handwritten stands out above email. If you work in the same office location, you can hand deliver it or leave it for them as a surprise on their desk.

- **Be mindful of what you say.** Regardless of whether you choose to send via email or handwrite the note, remember that others may see your note, so don't include anything you would consider confidential. If you want to thank them for something that needs to remain 100% confidential, I recommend doing so in person in a private setting (ex. your office, conference room, etc.).

- **Treat them!** Another idea is to take the team or individual out to lunch (and hopefully you will receive some follow up thank-you notes!) or dinner. Choosing dinner or lunch will depend on your team members. Some team members have obligations outside of the work day that will make it difficult or impossible to attend (for example, family/children) or they might not want to spend any time outside of office doing a "forced" work event.

- **Remember: Sometimes actions speak louder than words.** If you have the power, letting your employees leave a couple of hours early (paid, of course) is usually appreciated!

EXAMPLES:

Thanking the Team

Thank you to each of you for all of your hard work on [Project Name]. *Because of your extra efforts, we were able to meet the deadline.* [Client Name] *is very pleased with the presentation and promotion materials. You'll find some bagels and donuts for your enjoyment this morning. And we will plan a team lunch to celebrate soon!*

The productivity of our team during [Month of the Year] *exceeded the internal goal set by management. I thank all of you for focusing this month on the project work that mattered the most and contributed to revenue. The exercise we did on setting priorities was worthwhile and I appreciate that each one of you embraced the change. I am happy that you are on my team!*

The dedication this team has to each other is amazing. Once again, I watched you all pitch in and help each other to meet the goals for [Project]. *I was also impressed that you worked together to solve problems together and then presenting me with a list of possible solutions.*

Thank you, team, for coming together when we had the crisis with [Project/Customer Situation]. *I was impressed that all of you put in extra hours without complaining (at least not to me!) to get the work done to resolve the situations as quickly as possible. I spoke with*

[Boss's Name] *and she has approved for each of you to have two hours off on a day of your choosing. We will just need to coordinate to make sure you don't all choose the same day! Thanks again for your dedication.*

I appreciate the efforts of each you in the past year. I am proud of how you all pulled together as a team after the reorganization. You've proved that new teams can be successful quickly while working on [Project Name] *together. I am looking forward to the coming year and seeing how far we can go together. Keep up the good work!*

Your teamwork during the past week was very impressive. I am grateful for how all of you pulled together to get the work done for [Client Name]. *Because of your hard work, we've been able to secure the contract with* [Client Name] *for another year. Please enjoy donuts this morning and we will do a team lunch or happy hour as soon as the schedule allows for it.*

Thanking an Individual

Thank you for stepping up and leading the team while I was out unexpectedly. With your leadership, the projects stayed on track. I also received many compliments about how well you handled things from others on the team.

I was very impressed with you how you handled [Difficult Situation]. *Thank you for reassuring* [Client Name] *by sharing the details as to how we will solve the problem and the steps we will put in place to prevent this problem from occurring again. I am grateful for your easygoing manner that brings comfort to the customers and* [Client Name] *loves having you on their account.*

I appreciate all the time you've spent mentoring [Employee Name]. [She/He] *has told me how much better they understand their role because of your help. You've been able to show* [Him/Her] *how to use our internal programs that in a way that makes sense. I am grateful that you've helped her round out her skills.* [She/He] *is progressing nicely thanks to you!*

Your event planning skills are wonderful! Thank you for helping to organize the volunteer event last week. Everyone liked the event and the timing between the event and lunch worked out perfectly. I am grateful for the time you spent planning and working out the details with the [Volunteer Organization Name].

Thank you for volunteering to take on [New Initiative]. *With your years of experience, you are the perfect fit.* [Initiative Name] *is very excited to have you as part of the team. I hope it is a rewarding experience for you.*

I want to recognize your years of service with [Company Name]. [number of years] *years is admirable! While my tenure has been much shorter, I can say that this team is better because of you. Your skills with* [Program] *are exceptional and I appreciate that time you take to mentor the newer team members.*

ADMINISTRATIVE ASSISTANT

An administrative assistant may also be known as an administrative professional. They do a variety of tasks depending on who they are working for.

Administrative Assistant's Day is on the Wednesday of the last full week of April. Thanking your administrative assistant on that day is expected. Surprise your assistant by thanking them throughout the year!

Also, the administrative assistant does not need to be your own administrative assistant. This person could be an administrative assistant for your department or company. Also, their title may not exactly be administrative assistant, but their tasks are still similar.

You Can Thank Your Administrative Assistant For...

- **Doing their job well.** A good administrative assistant will keep things running smoothly!

- **Helping you out when in a bind.** At my current workplace, I have witnessed the administrative assistant helping people out of a tight spot with little notice.

- **Arranging the catering for an on-site event.** I bet you are glad you didn't have to do this yourself!

- **Managing your calendar.** This could be setting up meetings or limiting the number of meetings you attend.

- **Organizing an event that went very well.**

- **Remembering the important stuff,** like sending flowers on your behalf to your mom on her birthday.

- **Thank them for whatever they are doing that you appreciate!** Be sure to thank them for something specific!

Examples:

Thank you for helping me with [Task]. *Your knowledge and skills are impressive and make this task much easier. I appreciate the time you took out of your day to assistant me.*

Thank you for keeping the office running so well! I'm glad I don't have to think about the details of the office since you took over. I appreciate that people are coming to you first when an issue arises. You did a wonderful job resolving the issue with the air conditioning temperature level.

I am always impressed with your willingness to help me. I appreciate that you came to my rescue when I was having problems setting up the projector in the conference room. Your quick troubleshooting abilities allowed for the meeting to start on time.

Thank you for organizing the volunteer event at [Organization or Event Name] *for my team. The team had a great time and we were able to bond while volunteering. Your time was well spent lining this up for us.*

I want to let you know that I appreciate that you sent flowers on my behalf to my mom last week on her birthday. As you know I was traveling then and was not able to coordinate this myself. My mom loved the flowers! They made her day which made my day.

You are amazing! I am thankful for how well you have organized the files. It's so much easier to find things now. I like your system! Thank you for having the patience to set it up.

Thank you for helping me with the projector system last week. I am very glad that you were able to quickly solve the problem and we were able to show the slides to the customer. They made the difference as [Client Name] *liked what they saw and signed up for* [Product or Service Name]!

The cake you ordered for the boss's birthday was wonderful! Can you share your source? The way you had it decorated was perfect too. Your attention to detail is appreciated, even when it comes to cake! [Boss's Name] *seemed to be impressed too!*

Thank you for answering and screening my phone calls. I can trust your judgment with the calls I should take right away versus calling back later. Your process has saved me many hours of phone time as I can often follow-up with an email instead of a lengthy phone call. Also, thanks for getting me lunch last week when I forgot mine at home!

I am grateful for your daily support. The processes you have developed for my email are saving me hours every week. I have come to trust your judgment. Please let me know if you see other areas that could be improved!

THANK YOUR SMALL BUSINESS CUSTOMERS

IN THE SUMMER OF 2013, my husband and I purchased new bicycles from a local bike store. We stopped to see what they had, as they were advertising a bike sale. The salesperson encouraged me to test drive a bike. She knew what she was doing. The bike was the most comfortable bike I'd ever ridden and it was my favorite color (purple). I was sold. I made the impulse purchase and do not regret it!

A week or so later, we received a thank-you note in the mail. The inside of the card contained a generic printed message, but someone also wrote in their thanks and specifically mentioned the bikes. They also signed their name in real pen (I've seen other cards where names are part of the printed card).

Fast forward to the summer of 2014. We decided to buy some accessories for my bike. I wanted a rack for bags so that I could ride the bike to the grocery store and pick up groceries. A chain with a lock was also needed to secure the bike at the store. To keep track of my distance traveled and speed, I wanted an odometer/speedometer device. And also a mirror so I could see traffic behind me. (I already had a helmet, if you feel concerned about my safety.)

All of the accessories could have been purchased online for less than the prices at the local store. I suggested this frugal option to my husband. We discussed it and decided to make all bike accessory purchases at the local store. We felt like the local store appreciated our business because of the thank-you note.

We spent hundreds of dollars at the store due to a thank-you note that was a very small investment for them—a bit of time and the cost of the card. If the thank-you note had been entirely printed with nothing handwritten, it would have been a nice gesture but not as meaningful. It also probably wouldn't have been as effective.

Handwritten notes will work best for small business and where there is personal interaction when buying the item or service. Handwritten thank-you notes are also nice for online coaching programs where the number of students is limited.

For online purchases, I like it when there is a handwritten "thanks" or "thank you" from whoever put the items in the box. It makes me feel appreciated and helps me to recognize that a real person was involved in the process (meaning that the whole process was not 100% automated, even though it may feel that way).

Examples:

> *We appreciate your recent purchase of* [Item Name]. *We hope you are enjoying it. Please let us know if you have any questions.*

> *Thank you for enrolling in my coaching program! I am excited to have you. I look forward to seeing how your life has transformed by the end of the program.*

Thanks for depending on us for your car repairs and maintenance. Your dedication to regular oil changes has extended the life of your car. Let us know if you ever need anything!

Thank you for shopping at our online store! We hope you are loving your first purchase of [Item Name]. *We make it in small batches to improve the quality. Please use code* [Enter Code] *to save 10% on your next order!*

I felt happy when I saw that you signed up for [Program Name]. *Based on our interaction through email and the Facebook group, we will work well together. I look forward to helping you reach your goals.*

We are looking forward to being your donut supplier! Thank you for choosing us for your church programs. We look forward to providing you with the best donuts in town every week. If you have any special requests, please be sure to let us know.

Thank you for purchasing your bike from us. We want to let you know that one bike tune-up is included per year. We hope you love your new bike!

I am excited to have you in [Online Program]. *There will be about twenty others and I hope you have a chance to connect with some other others in addition to the 1:1 support from me. I am looking forward to seeing how the program helps you!*

Thank you for being our customer from the last five years. We look forward to serving you and your family for many years to come. And a huge thank-you for recommending us to so many of your friends and family.

We want to thank you for purchasing your tires with us. Free tire rotation is included for the lifetime of the tires. We appreciate that you trusted us to help you decide which tires were best for your car.

FOOD
RELATED

FOR FOOD AFTER SURGERY AND/OR A HOSPITAL STAY

IF YOU OR AN IMMEDIATE FAMILY member has been hospitalized or had surgery, you and your family may be receiving one or two meals a day for a few days or more. These meals could be from your church or other family members and friends. Preparing and delivering meals takes time and they are not free. Even if you receive pizza or a takeout meal, this still takes time, energy, and money on the part of the giver.

Bringing someone food is a way of showing love. Someone cared enough to bring you food. Take a few minutes to send a thank-you note to show your appreciation. The time needed to write the thank-you note will be much less than it took for the meal to be prepared and delivered.

Hopefully, the food that was provided was yummy. This will make it easier too. If you hated the food, that is unfortunate. In the latter situation, remember the thought and care behind the food is more important than the actual food. The goal is to be thankful for their efforts.

If you feel well enough to eat, you should also be able to keep a list of who brought you food and what it was. If the person visited with you for a bit when they dropped off the food record that too. In addition to the meal, you can thank them for visiting.

What if you are not well enough to eat? If there are other household members, they can keep track of the list. The food may actually be intended for them anyway. This happens when you are the one that usually prepares meals and are unable to cook while recovering from surgery or other illness.

Depending on your ailment, you may also want to write a thank-you note each day. This will keep them from adding up and you will not have to write many at the same time. If you are capable of reading while recovering, you should also have the mental capacity to write a thank-you note. Unless of course, your writing hand was the reason for the surgery!

Another person in the home could also write the thank-you notes. Especially when you are having days where you can't eat much or are too out of it to eat. Your spouse or children can write the thank-you notes too, as they are likely the main beneficiary of the food.

Remember to plan ahead when the surgery or hospital visit is planned. If you know you are going to be out of action for a bit and food will be delivered, purchase thank-you note cards before being incapacitated.

Examples:

> *We greatly appreciate the meal you brought us when [Name] had knee surgery. Those first few days were a little rough and I was happy to not need to worry about making meals. The mac and cheese you brought was comforting too!*

Thank you for making the wonderful chicken casserole for us. It is a blessing to not have to think about preparing meals while [Name] is recovering. The kids and I enjoyed the meal! [Name] also appreciated you visiting with her when you delivered the meal.

I heard you organized all the food for my family when I was incapacitated. I hope I never have pneumonia again! I appreciate that you took the lead and made sure that we had food every day. I thank you for the extra time you took to make sure my kids did not go hungry. I was worried about them when I woke up from the fever. It turns out they were just fine!

I am grateful for the time you spent with me when dropping off the [Dish] after my surgery. I am not used to being alone so much. Visiting with you made my day. I am happy to report that I will be back on my feet soon! I'll take you to lunch then.

Thank you for ordering pizza from the family last [Day of the Week]. The kids loved it. We don't order pizza often, so it felt like a treat. I am starting to feel better and look forward to seeing you at [Location] next week.

I am very thankful for the meals you dropped off last week. I liked all of them. The [Dish] was my favorite. Can you share the recipe? I am happy to share that I'm back on the feet and back to making our meals.

The [Dish] was wonderful! I will request to have you on the meal making list if I ever need another surgery. It tasted so good. Much better than anything from the restaurant. Thank you for taking the time to make it and bring it over.

Thank you for making meals for my family with short notice. The emergency [Medical Procedure] *that* [Name] *had was very overwhelming for me. I am grateful that my kids were able to have nutritious meals to eat. They are still raving about the chicken and gravy!*

I felt deeply touched that you remembered that breakfast is my favorite type of meal. The egg and hash brown casserole that you provided after my stay at the hospital was fantastic. And, the Pyrex dish was beautiful. I promise to return it soon!

Thank you for the homemade meals! [Name] *is still recovering and unable to stand long enough to cook. We didn't realize how much she did until* [Medical Procedure] *put her out of action. We enjoyed your* [Dish]. [Name] *was not able to have any of it as she was still on liquids only then. She is doing better now and would like the recipe as she thought the* [Dish] *looked great and the kids loved it.*

THANK-YOU NOTES
FOR DINNER

IF YOU'VE HAD DINNER at a friend's house or went to a dinner party, be sure to follow up with a thank-you note. First, I will share some reasons on why you should write a thank-you note for the dinner.

You Can Thank Your Dinner Host For...

- **Their time.** Making dinner takes a lot of time and organization. Most hosts clean their house extensively to have it ready for visitors.

- **Their hospitality.** The host opened up their home to you. They hosted a potluck for your group. They may not have had to prepare all (if any) of the food, but they still had you into their home.

- **The food.** To compliment them on a dish you enjoyed. You can also request the recipe in your note.

- **All of their effort.** If the host feels appreciated they are much more likely to do another dinner.

- **Respecting your diet.** The host followed your special diet (paleo, no sugar, nut allergy) or made your favorites. They didn't make anything you are allergic to or hate.

- **Gathering everyone together.** Eating together is about more than the food. It's about spending together, connecting, and building stronger relationships.

There is one exception: If you have a weekly meal with the same group of people, you do not need to write the host a thank-you note each time. Be sure to thank them in person before leaving each week. Then you can write them an occasional thank-you note.

When possible, my sister has me over for dinner about once a week. And my parents have my husband and me and my sister's family over for lunch nearly every Sunday. I say "thank you" each time but do not send a weekly thank-you note. I feel that a weekly thank-you note is over the top and eventually will just become routine and not meaningful.

Tips:

- **Tell them what you enjoyed most.** To make your dinner thank-you note awesome, mention something specific that you liked. Only saying "Thanks for dinner" will feel very generic. What exactly are you thanking them for? If you loved a particular dish tell them. If you met new friends at the dinner, thank the host for the introduction. Otherwise, recognize the amount of time it took them to prepare.

- **Remember the details.** Be sure to include any extra consideration your host showed you, like allergies, preferences, etc.

Template:

Dear [Insert name],

Thank you for dinner on [Insert day of the week]. I liked the [Insert your favorite dish]. [Insert one or more of the reasons listed above, phrased in your own words]. I hope we can share dinner again soon!

Thanks Again,

[Sign your name]

Examples:

Thank you for having me over for dinner last Tuesday. I enjoyed visiting with your family. And thank you for making a 21-day sugar detox friendly meal! The Brussels sprouts were fantastic.

I enjoyed the dinner at your house last Friday night. I am amazed with the amount of dishes that you made and they were all so wonderful. Thank you for spending so much time to prepare it. The grilled lamb chops were my favorite!

I was very impressed that you made a paleo meal for us. I hope you liked the meal as much as we did! We appreciate that you are giving paleo a chance. Next time we will have to our place for more paleo-inspired recipes!

Thank you for inviting [Spouse's Name] and me to your home for dinner. The pot roast and mashed potatoes were delicious. Your living room felt cozy with the fireplace during dessert. Next time, we will have you over to our place!

Thank you for dinner! Being invited over at the last minute was a welcomed surprise. I was so happy *not having to make something after work. You are a wonderful neighbor and friend. The chicken soup was amazing too!*

The dinner party was awesome last night! We had a great time eating, laughing, and visiting with the others. Your friend, [Name], is so funny! Where did you find the time to make all of that food? The walnut stuffed dates wrapped with bacon were one of the best things I have ever tasted! We are looking forward to the next party already!

We had a great time last weekend sharing dinner with your family. Thank you for inviting us! Your dining table is magnificent. Was it made by the local Amish family? The turkey and side sides were very tasty too. We also enjoyed visiting with your children and getting to know them better. They are delightful.

What is your secret to making so many homemade dishes at the same time? The dinner you prepared for us was wonderful. It was my first time to have Chinese dishes outside of a restaurant. The sweet and sour chicken was the best I've had. Thanks for including us in your dinner get together.

Thank you for dinner last week. I felt energized after the meal and discussion. I enjoy your family very much. I love hearing [Child's Name]'s stories. The one about the cat and the sink made my night.

The appetizers/finger food dinner party was super fun! Thank you for hosting it and for taking the time to make so many dishes! The [Dish] was my favorite! Can you please email me the recipe? I am looking forward to the next party. Food and friends are the best!

THANK-YOU NOTES FOR LUNCH

Lunch is an awesome opportunity to stay in touch with others, make new friends, take a break with a co-worker, and meet with business contacts. Lunch is often more casual than dinner.

Does every lunch situation require a thank-you note? Not always. In the situations below where I recommend not writing a thank-you note, you absolutely can still send a thank-you note if you want to. These are the guidelines I follow. You should do what you feel is right for you and your situation.

DO send a thank-you note after...

- **The boss buys your lunch.**

    If the co-worker is your boss, or if this was a team lunch with the boss, then I recommend following up with a thank-you note. Please refer to the chapter in this book about thanking your boss for lunch.

- **Lunch with a mentor.**

    The first time you have lunch with a mentor, I recommend writing them a thank-you note. This will let the person know you sincerely appreciate the help and advice they are giving you. It will also help emphasize the importance of your relationship with them. They took time out of their day to meet with you! And, yes, you should still write a thank-you note even when you paid for the mentor's lunch.

- **A birthday lunch.**

  Birthdays are special. Following up with a thank-you note is a wonderful way to recognize the celebration of your birthday. If you feel your relationship with whoever took you out is too casual for a handwritten thank-you note, then I recommend a thank-you email.

- **A Lunch Treat.**

  Did someone surprise you by taking you out for lunch? Did this treat make your day? Respond by sending the person a thank-you note. It may surprise them!

DO NOT send a thank-you note after…

- **The casual lunch with a friend.**

  For the casual lunch with a friend a thank-you note is not needed when one person treats the other, especially when you are rotating who pays for lunch. My friend Alice and I take turns buying each other lunch almost every week. We've had this tradition for nearly fifteen years. We are not writing thank-you notes to each other for this. That would be too many and they would lose their meaning. The exception may be when a friend takes you out for your birthday or treats you to an extra special lunch at a fancy restaurant.

- **A co-worker (not the boss) buys your lunch as a thank you.**

  What a nice gesture! This could be unexpected or planned. Perhaps, the co-worker is taking you to lunch to thank you for something with which you helped them. This type of lunch falls into the casual category and a thank-you note is not needed. I recommend thanking them verbally at the end of lunch or perhaps an email thank-you.

Examples:

Thank you for taking me to lunch at [Restaurant Name]. *I am grateful for our friendship and had fun at lunch. It was a nice treat for me and it made my day.*

I was very surprised that you took me to lunch! I enjoyed helping you at work and didn't expect this. I appreciate the recognition and I liked getting to know you a bit better during lunch.

Thank you for agreeing to have lunch with me. I am grateful for the advice you gave me around [Topic]. *I was also able to relate to your story about how you got started with* [Topic].

I learned a great deal about [Topic] *at lunch last week. I appreciate the time you took out of your day to meet with me. I've already begun to take action on your advice. I will send you a follow up email in a couple of weeks describing the results I've had.*

Thank you for the lunch treat! [Restaurant Name] *is one of my favorites. I had a nice time catching up with you as well. We should do this more often.*

I love our birthday lunch tradition! Thank you for taking me to [Restaurant Name] *for my birthday lunch this year.*

Thanks for lunch! I had a wonderful time chatting. I was excited to learn that we both love [Shared Interest]. *I will treat you to lunch next time and we can continue our discussion.*

Thanks for treating me to lunch. That was a welcome surprise as you know my budget is tight lately and I love going out to eat. I had a nice time and look forward to seeing you again soon.

Thank you for the lunch. I enjoyed hearing about what has been going on in your life lately. We should catch up more often. Let's plan to have lunch at least once a month going forward.

Thank you for the birthday lunch. I look forward to it each year. I was surprised that you took me to [Restaurant Name]! *It's so fancy! I loved every minute of it and the bacon wrapped scallops were great.*

PRIMARY FOOD PROVIDER

In most families, one person is the primary maker of meals. This could be a spouse or parent or other relative. Making homemade meals is time consuming—and then there is the cleanup time for washing dishes and putting away leftovers. Sometimes, it can feel like a thankless job. I admit that I did not appreciate all the effort and time my mom spent making meals until I moved out and was responsible for my own.

Saying "thank you" after the meal is nice but can begin to feel very routine and meaningless. An occasional thank-you note is a thoughtful gesture to let them know they are appreciated.

Tips:

- **You don't have to write a note every night.** Obviously, writing and sending a thank-you note after every meal is impractical. But sending a note every now and then is very nice.

- **Give them a night off!** Go out for dinner or take a turn making the meal and doing the cleanup. Even helping with the cleanup is a blessing. I am always thankful when my husband does the dishes!

Examples:

Thank you for providing wonderful homemade meals for the family. I know that sometimes they can take a while to make. Please know that I appreciate them as they provide energy and taste great! The shrimp dish you made last week was fantastic!

I love the meals that you prepare! Perhaps, you can start teaching me and I can help out sometimes. I would love to be able to give you a break some nights. Can we start with something easy?

Thank you for taking the time to make our meals and have enough leftovers for me to take to work the next day. Your meals are so much better than the frozen single serve meals we used to rely on. I understand that all the cooking can be a lot of work and time. It's worth it. You are amazing and I love you for caring enough to make healthy food for us.

Thank you for cooking for me! I would not be eating healthy food if you didn't take the time to make it for us. I appreciate all the time you spend meal planning, grocery shopping, and making the recipes.

Happy New Year! I figured out that you prepared over 1,000 meals at home for us last year. That is a lot of cooking. I love your food and thank you for making things homemade. I have the best packed lunch in my class at school.

Please consider this a coupon for a complete day off from cooking. We can go out or I will make the meals that day. I appreciate all you do for the family and would like to give you a break. I know one day isn't much, but it's a start.

You are the best cook ever! Thank you for making our meals every day. Can you teach me how to make a few of the easier dishes? I liked to be prepared when I leave home.

Thank you for caring for the family. We can see your love in the dishes you prepare as they are all healthy and nourishing. They are delicious and we are thankful that you are able to be a stay-at-home mom and also the chef of the house.

I love your food! Thank you for making me food every day. I want to start taking a turn every now and then. How about I start cooking every Saturday? I appreciate all you do and would like to cook at least one meal a week for you.

You are fantastic at making meals! The beef, bacon, and veggie casserole is one of my favorites. I know it takes a while for you to make it, but I sure do love it. Thank you for providing the meals.

Holidays

VALENTINE'S DAY

ARE YOU LOOKING for a different Valentine's Day Idea this year? How about thanking your Valentine? It can be as simple as including a sentence or two in their Valentine's Day card. Most Valentine's cards come with a printed verse in them. You can write your message on the other side (if it is a folded card) or above or below the verse.

Adding "I love you" is easy and expected to be added to the card. Adding gratitude will be a surprise. A good surprise.

Tips:

- **Show your appreciation.** When sending to a friend, it's a chance to let them know that you are glad they are in your life. How often do people tell their friends that their friendship is appreciated?

- **Say a little more.** If you are sending out Valentine postcards, adding a thank you is a way to say something along with Happy Valentine's Day.

EXAMPLES:

SPOUSE/SIGNIFICANT OTHER

Choose a message that is appropriate for your relationship. Otherwise, use these examples as inspiration to come up with your own personal message. Think about your relationship. Pick something that will be meaningful to your husband, wife, partner, boyfriend, girlfriend, etc. Looking at examples is fine to get ideas. For best results choose something that fits your relationship.

> *Thank you for all the ways you love me.* (You could also choose to be specific and name something that makes you feel loved.)
>
> *Thank you for loving me even when I'm crabby.*
>
> *Thank you for supporting the family so that I can stay home with the children.*
>
> *Thank you for showing me how much you love me. I appreciate things that appear to go unnoticed, like packing my lunch and having a meal ready when I come home from work.*
>
> *Thank you for supporting my new ideas.*
>
> *Thank you for being committed to date nights throughout the year.*

FRIEND

Thank you for being part of my life.

Thanks for being my friend.

Thanks for all the lunches we have shared this year!

Thanks for being there for me whenever I need a friend

(Remember, the more specific the note the more memorable it will be.)

BOSS AND COWORKERS

If you are only giving a Valentine to your boss, you may be viewed as sucking up. You will be less likely to be viewed as a suck up if you give a valentine to your entire team or other co-workers. It could be fun to pass out classroom Valentine's at work! If you are your boss's only employee, then a Valentine to just him/her would be fine.

> *Thank you for making our team great!*
>
> *I'm thankful that we are on the same team.*
>
> *I am grateful that we've become friends while working together.*
>
> *Thank you for helping me with the* [Project Name].

VALENTINE'S DAY GIFT THANK-YOU NOTES

REMEMBER THAT THIS is a thank-you note for a specific gift. Even though it was for Valentine's Day, it does not need to be turned into a love note. Love notes are great. Feel free to include a love note on separate note paper or as part of the thank you.

Don't be overly creative. Use words you would use if speaking to the person in real life. No need to get out your thesaurus. Express in your own words why you are thankful for the gift.

Tips:

- **Voice your gratitude.** If you live with the person that gave you the gift, a verbal thanks is probably sufficient to show your gratitude. However, if you desire, you can still write them a thank you.

- **Name the gift specifically.** Only saying "Thank you for the Valentine's Day gift" will leave them wondering if you remember what they gave you.

- **If appropriate, use "I Love you" or "Love" as the closing.** Including "Love" will not be appropriate for a co-worker, boss, teacher, or student.

- **Be yourself when writing your note** and substitute words as needed.

- **You can use any thank-you note card, but you may want to use a heart or love themed card for Valentine's Day.** Or any card with a picture that you like (or the receiver will like) that is blank on the inside.

- **Show some love.** Include an additional sentence that is appropriate based on your relationship with the giver. It can be to declare your love or thanking them for being your friend.

Template:

> *Dear* [Insert name],
>
> *Thank you for the* [Insert the gift] *for Valentine's Day. The* [Insert the gift] *is awesome. I will think of you when using it* [and be reminded of your love — if appropriate].
>
> [Closing*],
>
> [Sign your name]

* The closing will need to be adjusted depending on who you are thanking. For family members or significant others, "Love" is fine, otherwise go with "Sincerely," "Best Regards," or another closing of your choosing.

Examples:

> *Thank you for the Valentine's Day treat. I will have fun spending the money on something I enjoy soon. We also liked the stickers you used on the envelope.*

> *Thank you for the little box of chocolates for Valentine's Day. My sweet tooth appreciates them. I am glad we are on the same team!*

> *Thank you for giving me roses for Valentine's Day. They look and smell amazing sitting on my desk. I will think of you and our love whenever I see them.*

> *I am excited about the movie tickets! As you know, I've been wanting to see [Movie Name] for several weeks. I am looking forward to seeing it with you on our next date night! Thank you for remembering that I mentioned this movie.*

> *The box of candy is amazing! Where did you find one that is all dark chocolate? I appreciate that you paid attention to the details when I was describing my likes and dislikes when it comes to chocolate.*

> *Thank you for taking me out for dinner for Valentine's Day. And I was grateful that you planned ahead and made reservations at [Restaurant Name]. The crème brulee was excellent and made the night feel like magic.*

> *I was very surprised that we visited the new cat café on Valentine's Day. What a treat! I enjoyed the cats and know that our purchases will help support them until they can find their forever home. I love you for loving cats.*

Thank you for the best Valentine's Day yet! I was very surprised that you took the day off so that we could spend the day together doing the activities that you planned. We should make this an annual tradition. The zoo was my favorite part of the day.

I enjoyed our date on Valentine's Day. Thank you for the picnic at [Location Name]. *Avoiding the crowded restaurants was very thoughtful.*

Thank you for spending Valentine's Day with my kids! The kids had a great time at the water park and it made them feel special since I was not able to get the time off from work. They are still excited about the stuffed animal souvenirs. Now, they are hoping to spend Valentine's Day with you every year!

MOTHER'S DAY

THIS YEAR, I ENCOURAGE YOU to write your mom a thank-you note for Mother's Day. This can be done in addition to any other gifts that you may have planned for her. Our moms brought us into this world! Your mom may look at the note again and again. It may become a keepsake that she holds dear.

I have a wonderful mom. I am not a mother. The examples and ideas in this section are based on things for which I think moms would like to be thanked. If you are a mom, I suggest thinking about what you would like to be thanked for. If your mom also did those things, thank your mom for them. After all, you likely learned them from her!

You Can Thank Your Mom For…

- **Her Time.** Thank her for all the time she has spent with you and possibly your children. Has she been the go-to last minute babysitter? Does she help you whenever you need it? Does she drop everything to help you with your kids when they are sick or in trouble? Does she give you a ride when you need it? Does she let you borrow her vehicle?

- **Bringing you into this world.** You would not be here without your mom! I am fortunate to be alive as I was born six weeks early and came out breech. I have a twin brother. He stayed with mom and I was sent with Dad to another hospital for a week. And they had to care for our two older siblings. This was not an easy time for my parents.

- **Choosing you.** If you are adopted, you can thank her for choosing you. You were handpicked!

- **Being a good mom.** This was on my mom's list when I asked what she would like to be thanked for by her children. The criteria for what makes a "good" mom will vary as we all have our own perspectives. If you think your mom was a "good" mom, be sure to mention it.

- **Sick visits/help.** Did she sit with you while you were in the ER? Did she drive hours to help you when your child was very sick? When you are sick, does she pick-up your favorite beverage (got to stay hydrated!) and bring it over? Does she watch your kids when they are sick so that you do not have to take off from work? When you, your spouse, or child, were in the hospital did she visit?

- **Food.** Since I've taken up cooking and ditched almost all processed food, I've come to appreciate the amount of time, energy, and planning that goes into home cooked meals. Growing up, my mom was the primary preparer of our meals. We did not go out to eat very much and Mom had dinner on the table when Dad came home from work. My mom still makes Sunday lunch for our family each week! Food shared with others is a blessing. The hands that prepared it should be thanked. If your dad did/does most of the cooking, then be sure to thank him on Father's Day!

- **Packing your lunch.** My mom packed 99% of my lunches for school and work until I was 25. I admit that I was a little spoiled in this area. I didn't really appreciate the amount of time and planning to make lunches until I had to make my own! She was also making lunch for all other family members living at home and herself. For a few years, that was up to seven lunches a day. That's a lot of lunches. An effort that is worthy of being recognized even years later.

- **Being your friend.** I call my mom at least a few times a week. She's not only my mom but my friend! If you have a great relationship with your mom, thank her for it.

- **Taking an interest in your adult life.** You are an adult now and she still wants to know what is going on in your life and your kids'. I do not have any kids, but she often asks about my husband and our cats.

- **Unconditional Love.** She loves you no matter what you've done. You've made mistakes. She has helped you even if you went against her advice and things didn't turn out well. She still loved you even when you lied (perhaps, when you were a teenager) and then you got caught.

- **Playing games with you.** My mom taught my siblings and me to play Scrabble. It was one of our favorite games growing up and we still play it together. The game was fun, but also meant that she was spending time with us. And it turns out that maybe she made up some rules!

- **Coming to your sporting events.** When I attend my nephew's baseball games, there is usually not a parent there for every kid that is playing. That may be impossible for some parents due to work or other circumstances. If your mom was able to be there, thank her for coming. If she comes to your kids' events, thank her for that too.

The ideas above are just that. You know your mom best and what you should be thanking her for.

Tips:

- **I suggest handwriting the thank-you note.** If you do, your mom will be able to keep the note if she chooses. You can also pick out a card design that she will like. Also, it will feel more personal and permanent than an email. If you are buying a Mother's Day card, your note can be written inside the card or on a separate piece of paper or stationery.

- **Share what is in your heart.** This note can be longer than a typical thank-you note.

Templates:

Dear [Insert Mom, or however you refer to your mother],

[Insert something you are currently thankful for. Be as specific as possible.]

[Insert something from growing up or as a teenager. Something that you probably took for granted and did not appreciate at the time. Be as specific as possible.]

[Add a summary thank-you like *"Thanks for everything"* or *"Thanks for all you do"* or *"You are the best mom ever"* or *"I could not have asked for a better mother."* Pick something that feels true and not cheesy.]

Happy Mother's Day!

Love,

[Sign your name]

Shorter Version:

If a long thank-you note feels like too much, that's fine too. Focus on current events that you can thank her for. Perhaps your mom was not a "good" mom growing up but is now, focus on the present.

Dear [Insert Mom, or however you refer to your mother],

[Insert two or three sentences about something you are currently thankful for. Be as specific as possible.]

Happy Mother's Day!

Love,

[Sign your name]

Remember to keep thanking your mom all year. When she does nice things for you, send her a thank-you or find another way to thank her. You do not need to save a list for Mother's Day!

Examples:

Dear Mom,

Happy Mother's Day! I've been reflecting on all the things you've done for me during my life and want to thank you. Thank you for being a good mom. You were there for me when I was growing up and continue to support me in my adult life.

I also appreciate the unconditional love and support, even when I made mistakes and you tried to warn me. I should have taken your advice. I enjoy talking with you throughout the week. And I am thankful for the cooking tips and questions answered as I have tried out new recipes and cooking techniques.

Thanks for everything you do.

Love,

Heidi

Dear Mom,

I want to thank you for all the food you have prepared for me since you brought me into this world. From finding the right formula that I could digest to packing my lunch while I lived at home. And now, you continue to bless us with Sunday lunch. I am thankful for all the homemade meals and the time spent with family at the dinner table.

Also, thank you for all the times you have helped out when I've been sick. I really didn't think I was going to make it after I had my wisdom teeth out in high school. I felt like I was going to go crazy from the medicine.

You are a wonderful mother not only to me but to my siblings and their kids as well. Thanks for all you do.

Happy Mother's Day!

Love,

Heidi

Thank you for helping me out so much lately. I appreciate that you've come to my aid when I needed a ride to pick up my car. I have been enjoying our monthly lunches at [Restaurant Name].

I am so thankful that you are my mom. I am glad that you chose to adopt me and I feel like I could not have asked for a better mother. I love you very much and appreciate all that you have done for me.

Thank you for coming to my baseball games. The weather this year has been cold and rainy. Other moms have chosen to stay home, but you've come to every home game regardless of the weather. I appreciate your support. And thanks for packing me pre-game snacks.

I want to thank you for always being there for me during the last few months. These kidney stones have been brutal, and I appreciate you taking me to the emergency room. And I was glad you made some meals for me and helped with my dog. I will be so happy when the last stone passes!

Thank you for being my friend. I found out how many friends were not really true friends when I became pregnant. I feel like you are the only one who still wants to hang out with me! I am grateful for the time you've spent taking me to doctor's appointments when [Father's Name] *has been working.*

Have I ever told you how thankful I am for the upbringing you provided? I admit that I didn't really appreciate how many things you did for me until I had my own children! I didn't know packing lunches every day could take so long! Thank you for always making my lunches for me when I was at home.

The weekly game nights we've been having have been very fun. The kids enjoy spending time with their grandma and, of course, I like catching up with you and Dad. Thank you for providing the treats too! You are a wonderful mother.

Another year has passed and I have grown to appreciate you as my mother even more. I've learned so much from you about [Subject] *in the last year. I also am thankful that we live close enough to each other to have weekly visits. You are a blessing in my life!*

FATHER'S DAY

I ENCOURAGE YOU TO WRITE your dad a thank-you note for Father's Day. It could be better than any gift and make this Father's Day his best Father's Day ever! The thank-you note can be included in his Father's Day card or be a separate note.

Unless he was/is a terrible father, there is likely some reason you could show him gratitude and appreciation with a thank-you note. A handwritten note will be much more meaningful than just saying "thanks" in person.

You Can Thank Your Dad For...

- **Raising you.** While growing up, we often do not realize how much our parents do for us. If you are a parent now, you likely understand.

- **Special memories.** Did your dad spend time with you doing activities that you both enjoyed? I remember going fishing and making home bread (before there were bread machines!) with my father.

- **Continuing to support you as an adult.** Trying something new? Made some mistakes? Dad doesn't make you feel bad about it.

- **Giving you stuff from his garden.** My dad shares his bounty with my husband and me every year. Gardening is hard work and it only takes a moment to share the fruit of his labor.

- **Coming to the rescue whenever you are in need.** Have you ever run out of gas? Was it dad that came to your rescue?

- **Coming to your softball games when you were in high school.** I appreciated this and I am not sure if I ever told my dad thanks back when I was a teenager.

Choose a reason that comes from your heart and is true. It doesn't need to be complicated. Do not thank him for something you wished he would have done but never happened!

Tips:

- **Pick a thank-you note card design that your Dad** will like or is a basic design (just has 'thank you' on the front). If your dad does not like cats (my dad doesn't), don't use a thank-you note card with cats on it. Make this card 100% about your Dad!

- **Sound like yourself.** I call my father "Dad." My opening will be, "Dear Dad." In your note, refer to your father as you do in everyday life (Dear Papa, Father, Padre, etc.)

- **Name something specific** (use ideas above to brainstorm). If your note is super generic, for example, *"Dear Dad, Thanks for being my Dad, Happy Father's Day,"* then it will not be very meaningful. Write something that cannot be found in a standard Father's Day card.

- **Consider using "Happy Father's Day" as the closing.** That may sound predictable, but it is the one time a year that this closing works!

Examples:

I want to thank you for sharing vegetables with me every year from your garden. They taste great and are so full of flavor being so fresh. All of your gardening efforts also help me to save a little on groceries during the summer.

I don't think I have ever properly thanked you for coming to my softball games when I was in high school. At the time, I didn't appreciate your support as much as I do now looking back. Now that I have a job myself, I realize that it's not always easy or possible to leave work early to watch your kid play a sport. I am thankful that you made the effort even though I wasn't a very good player. I was happy to see you in the stands still wearing your business suit.

Thanks for another year of supporting my business ideas. I appreciate that you continue to listen to my ideas and encourage me to try new things. I would have given up by now without your ongoing support. It means a lot to me. Thank you for being a great dad and friend.

You are a wonderful father. Thank you for bringing me gas several times in the last few months. I have started watching the miles since we determined that the gas gauge is faulty. I hope you have a great Father's Day!

Thank you for being a man of integrity. Now that I am on my own, I appreciate your example of hard work and honesty while I was growing up. I am a better person because of what you taught my siblings and me.

Now that I have my own kids, I'm continuing the tradition of attending [Team Name] *games at least once a month during the summer. Going to games with you was one of my favorite memories when I was growing up. Thank you for starting that tradition. I hope my kids will appreciate as much as I do now.*

Thank you for being my friend and a great father. I appreciate all the help you've given with the boys since [Spouse's Name] *has passed away. The boys like the new routine with you picking them up from school. I am grateful to have you be a positive influence in their life.*

I have enjoyed the extra time we have spent together fishing and hunting over the past few months. Doing these things reminds me of my childhood. And now I understand the bond that can be built even when we are not talking.

Thank you for being my dad. I should tell you how much I appreciate you more than once a year! I appreciate our relationship and that I can come to you with anything. And I apologize for giving you so much grief when I was a teenager!

You've been a great example to me these last few months. You've inspired me to give up drinking. If you can do it, I can do it too. And it should be easier if we are encouraging each other not to drink. Thank you for your inspiration. It will be hard, but I believe we can become sober.

THANKSGIVING DAY

MOST PEOPLE CELEBRATE THANKSGIVING by gathering together with friends and family and having a Thanksgiving Day meal (aka feast). I usually celebrate with my family for lunch and then with my in-laws for dinner on Thanksgiving Day. Other families may have their meal on Friday (if they're not shopping!), Saturday or Sunday.

If you went to someone else's home (even if it was your parents) for Thanksgiving, I recommend sending the host a thank-you note to show your gratitude.

You Can Thank The Thanksgiving Host Family For...

- **Making all the food**, like my mom did (thanks mom!). Feeding ten, twenty, or more people is not free! Preparing that much food also takes many hours. It's not easy having everything all ready at the same time. Crock pots can help with this!

- **Cleaning and preparation.** They will (hopefully) have cleaned their house.

- **Cleaning after the meal.** They are likely the ones that will be washing the dishes. (It is appreciated if you offer to help with clean up!)

- **Giving their time.** They may be missing the football game they really wanted to watch to have you at their house.

- **Being great hosts.** They invited you into their home.

- **Being considerate.** They may have had to make special arrangements for their pets. If they have big dogs, perhaps they had to board them in a kennel. If you are allergic to cats, perhaps they kept their cats sequestered in a bedroom.

- **Making you something special.** They may have made your favorite Thanksgiving dish that they do not like themselves. I have a hard time making food that I do not like!

- **Gathering everyone together.** You were able to see other members of your extended family.

- **Cooking!** It takes work to make a meal, especially one as big as on Thanksgiving!

The thank-you note will show the host family that their efforts are appreciated.

Tips:

- **Tell them what you enjoyed most.** Remember the best thank-you note tip is to name something specific in your note that you appreciated.

- **Keep it short and sweet.** This is an occasion worthy of a three or four-sentence thank-you note.

- **Look ahead.** If you will see them at Christmas, you can mention that you are looking forward to seeing them in a few weeks.

- **Be tactful.** If you hated a dish, don't mention that one. Pick a dish that you enjoyed to compliment.

Examples:

Thank you for having us over for Thanksgiving and for preparing all of the food. My favorite dish was the corn casserole. We also enjoyed spending time with you and the family.

Thank you for having [Me/Us] over for Thanksgiving. [Reason for Being Thankful]. I look forward to seeing you again in December.

We enjoyed the Thanksgiving get-together. Thank you for hosting this year. The fall-themed tablecloth and matching napkins were perfect. We all think your mashed potatoes are the best! What is your secret to getting them so creamy? The boys want me to learn how to make them that way. We all had a delightful visit with the family. We will see you at the New Year's Eve party!

I was very impressed with the vegetarian dishes you made for Thanksgiving dinner. I didn't expect that and appreciated your efforts. The bean dish was amazing, as well as the Brussels sprouts. Thank you for honoring my way of eating in your home.

I was very happy to see the family at the Thanksgiving dinner. I found it special that Aunt [Name] and Uncle [Name] were able to come this year. Your long dining table is a blessing when family gets together as we can all fit around the same table. Thank you for providing your home as a way for us to all see each other.

I was so happy that you made [Dish] for Thanksgiving. I don't understand how you can hate it! I felt loved seeing it on the table as I find it difficult to make things I do not like to eat, and that is exactly what you did for me.

Thank you for hosting Thanksgiving dinner again this year. We appreciate that you kept your cats in the bedroom as it helps with [Name]'s allergy. We had a nice time visiting with the family and look forward to seeing everyone at our house for Christmas.

We had a nice time on Thanksgiving! I am grateful that I was able to just show and not have to make anything. The dishes you made were wonderful and I am very impressed that they were all ready at the same time. Also, your new kitchen looks like something from HGTV. [Name] did a great job with the remodel. Maybe he can do my kitchen next!

Thank you for hosting Thanksgiving again this year. I know how much work it can be to clean and prepare food. We love how cozy your house is and, of course, the boys enjoyed watching the football game.

I appreciate your family for inviting me to Thanksgiving dinner since I was not able to travel home to be with my family this year. I enjoyed meeting your extended family and had an interesting chat with [Name]. He has inspired me to take more risks with all of his adventure stories from his younger years.

CHRISTMAS

Many gifts are given and received at Christmas. But that does not mean we shouldn't show our gratitude! Plan to write a thank-you note for the Christmas gifts you receive to show your appreciation.

Q&A:

Should children living at home with their parent(s) or caretaker write thank-you notes to them? No, this is not necessary. The kids can give verbal thanks for their gifts when living with the parents. Of course, they still can write a note if they want to, but parents do not need to ask them to do so. I confirmed this with family members who have children.

Who should you thank for Christmas gifts? Anyone who gave you a gift that lives outside of your home. This could be friends, aunts, uncles, grandparents, other family members, boss, employees, co-workers, etc.

Should you write a thank-you note for a Christmas card? No. If you receive a card in the mail, you do not need to write a thank-you note for it. If you receive money or a gift card in the card, you NEED to send your thanks, but if it is only a card or card with a Christmas letter, you do not need to reciprocate with a thank-you note.

My younger children received Christmas gifts but are not old enough to write their own note. Should I write the note for them? Yes. A thank-you note will acknowledge that the gift was appreciated. If you have multiple children, one thank-you note from the entire family is fine.

Does the thank-you note need to be handwritten? Yes. Handwritten notes are more personal. It will very likely take less time to write the thank-you note than it took the person to pick up the gift for you. However, if you have a reason for not handwriting it, please at least send an email or text message. That's better than no acknowledgment at all.

We did a white elephant gift exchange at the Christmas party. Should we write thank-you notes? No. Depending on how the game is played, you may not know who the gift was from. Also, white elephant gift items are usually not expensive (they could be something from home you just didn't want), could be goofy, and not personally picked out for you. So unless the dollar amount for the gifts was high, skip the thank-you notes. The exchange is more about the fun of the exchange than what you end up with.

The people I exchange Christmas gifts with never send thank-you notes. Should I still send them a thank-you note? Yes. They may not know how to write a note or are not in the routine, or perhaps they have some other reason. You can still send them one.

What if I do not like the gift and will not be keeping it? You should still write a thank-you note. Try your best to be polite, without lying. Don't say you love it when you don't.

Thank them for the gesture of giving you a gift. Depending on your relationship with the person you may be able to tell them or make a joke about re-gifting it.

Tips:

- **Do double-duty.** If your birthday is within seven to ten days of Christmas (either before or after) you can write one thank you that includes your birthday and Christmas gifts to those who gave you both. Your note will need to be a little longer than most thank-you notes as you will need to specifically mention all of the birthday and Christmas gifts.

- **Write the note within one to two weeks of when you received the gift.** Aim to do them as soon as possible. If you received the gift in the mail and are not sending the note within one or two days, I suggest sending an email or contacting the giver in some way to let them know it was received. Then you can follow up with a thank-you note. If you are not prompt in acknowledging the gift, the giver is left to wonder if the card or gift got lost in the mail.

- **Help your older kids keep track of what they are receiving.** This is extremely helpful if they are getting gifts at different Christmas parties. Use a notebook or small notepad to make the list.

- **Be organized and plan ahead for thank-you note writing.** If you have thank-you notes on hand before receiving gifts, you are much more likely to write them promptly. If you are reading this after Christmas, that's okay. Pick up some cards when you can.

- **Use a Christmas-themed note card, if you want to.** If not, pick a nice looking thank-you note card that the receiver will like. More tips are choosing the design can be read in the chapter dedicated to choosing the design of a card. For quality note cards, I recommend Current Catalog and Minted. If you do not mind sifting through reviews to find quality cards, Amazon has plenty of choices. Suzy's Zoo and Lang are two brands on Amazon that I have used and are quality items.

- **If you attend a Christmas party, send the host a thank-you note.** Generally, parties are a lot of work, time to plan and organize, and make or arrange for food.

Template:

Dear [insert name],

Thank you for the [insert gift]. [Next, specifically say how you will use it, why you like it, what you are going to spend the money on, etc.] [Then add a comment about the holiday party or seeing them, etc.]

Thanks Again,

[Sign your name]

EXAMPLES:

Family/Friends

Thank you for giving us Apples to Apples for Christmas. We enjoyed playing this game with you last summer and we are very happy to have our own copy. We can play it the next time you are over. We hope you had a nice Christmas.

Thank you for Scrabble along with the Scrabble Dictionary! This is one of our favorite games and we look forward to playing many games. We look forward to seeing you every year at the annual Christmas party.

Thank you for The Hunger Games book set. I liked the movies and I will look forward to reading the books. I had a nice time visiting with you at the holiday party and hope to see you soon.

Thank you for sending us some Christmas cash. We will be putting it towards a new microwave. As you know, we've been without one for quite a while now and look forward to the convenience of having one again. We are excited to see you soon at the family Christmas party!

Thank you for the Christmas money. I will be saving it for something fun, perhaps a nice dinner out or to see a movie. I enjoyed playing games with you at the party and catching up. I was happy to hear that your children are doing well.

Your Christmas party was awesome! Thanks so much for having us over. It was a nice surprise to see the Jones's there as we have not seen them in many years. The food was great too. I love that you had chips and homemade guacamole, one of my favorites. I look forward to seeing you again soon.

Thank you for having us over for Christmas. We enjoyed the food and visiting with the family. It is always a joy to spend time at your home. Your children are delightful and we like playing games with them.

Work

Thank you for the Christmas bonus. I look forward
to it each year and was very excited with the amount
I received. I am thankful for your and the company's
generosity. I hope you enjoy your time off for the holidays!

Thank you for the Christmas bonus. It was unexpected
and will allow my family to have a few extra gifts this
Christmas! I am thankful to work on your team and
at a company where hard work is rewarded. I hope you
have a great Christmas!

Thank you for the team out to lunch for Christmas.
Having a fancy lunch with the team was fun. I also
appreciate that you reserved a private room at the
restaurant for us. I hope you have a great Christmas!

Thank you for the Christmas team lunch. Chatting with
you and the team away from the office was enjoyable.
And of course, the food was wonderful. I hope you have
a wonderful Christmas!

Thank you for the gift card to [Store Name]. I love
shopping there and I will use it towards some new clothes
for work. We will miss seeing you at the Christmas party
this year, but understand that you will be working.

EVENTS

BIRTHDAY

HAPPY BIRTHDAY! Congratulations on making it another year. Since you are reading this chapter, I'm assuming you want to thank those that gave you gifts.

Tips:

- **Don't forget the event.** A birthday thank-you note is similar to any thank-you for a gift, only you'll want to include "birthday" in your note to acknowledge that was the event for which you received it.

- **Say thanks for coming.** If you had a party, you can also use the note as a way to acknowledge the giver's presence.

Examples:

Thank you for [Gift] *for my birthday. I will* [Use/ Enjoy/Read/Listen—choose the appropriate verb] [to] *it soon. I was excited that you remembered how much I like* [Subject]. [I also thank you for coming to the party — if you had a party].

Thank you for the money for my birthday! I will be spending it on lunches out while at the office. I usually pack my lunch every day, so going out will be a real treat for me!

I enjoyed seeing you at my birthday party. I appreciate that you found a wine made in the year I was born. I will be saving the bottle after we drink the wine.

I love the cat coloring book that you gave me for my birthday. I had no idea that adult coloring books are very popular now. This book is perfect for me given my love of cats! I am looking forward to coloring while I watch TV in the evenings. Thank you!

Thank you for sharing my birthday with me. I also appreciate the gift card to [Restaurant Name]. *Your dad and I like to go there at least once a week.*

I am thankful for the time we had together on my birthday! Dinner out at [Restaurant Name] *was a surprise. I had fun and enjoyed our conversation. I will be sure to take you out on your birthday this year!*

Thank you for the blanket you made for me for my birthday. The design is beautiful and your sewing abilities are amazing. I will treasure the blanket for years to come! [Name] *has hinted that he would like one of your homemade blankets too!*

The cat earrings you picked out for me are perfect. They are cute and as you know, I don't think all cat items are cute! I will wear these earrings often as they are adorable. They remind me of my cat, [Name].

Thank you for coming to my 40th birthday party! You were a lot of fun at the party. Everyone loves your jokes and storytelling. Thank you for making the party great.

Thank you for spending the day with me on my birthday! I had fun at the zoo and dinner afterward was great as well. I enjoyed spending the day with you and I'm grateful for you giving me the gift of your time.

GRADUATION

WHETHER YOU'VE GRADUATED from high school, college, or any other academic or training program, it is important to show your appreciation to those who honored you on the day.

HIGH SCHOOL GRADUATION

If you have a child (or children) graduating high school, they will need to write thank-you notes for any gifts that they receive. If you are a parent reading this, your child may need your help to get organized and not feel overwhelmed by the task. Your attitude could impact how much they enjoy or do not enjoy the process. Being prepared will hopefully lead to less nagging to get your graduate to finish the thank-you notes.

Tips:

- **Help your graduate get started.** If your child did not grow up writing thank-you notes for birthday and holiday gifts, they might need some help to get started with knowing what to say. The examples below can help. If they've been writing thank-you notes already, it will be easier for them. The difference will be that they will have more to write at one time than usual.

- **Stay organized when opening gifts.** Make a list of who gave each gift and what the gift was as it is opened. Remember to keep track of gifts received in the mail too! Perhaps a parent or another family member can make the list while the graduate opens each gift. Record the gift giver's name and the gift. If a list is not made, they will likely feel frustrated when it is time to write the notes and can't remember who gave what. Do not convince yourselves that you/they will remember! Do you remember what you had for lunch three days ago?

- **Involve the graduate early.** Let them help choose the thank-you note design. They may get excited about the thank-you note process if the design of the card is to their personal taste.

- **Share the space.** I have a twin brother and we had a joint high school graduation party. This was another opportunity where we were able to share thank-you note cards. For people that gave us both a gift, I wrote my thank-you note on one side of the card and my brother used the other. We had to be careful to make sure we didn't write the same message! This approach also allowed my parents to save a bit on the cost of thank-you note cards and stamps.

Examples:

Thank you for coming to my graduation party and for

the cash. I appreciate it and will be saving it for when I start college in the fall. I will put it in my fund to cover the costs of books as I hear they can be expensive.

I am thankful for the gas gift cards. They will be great when I'm on my own and having to buy all of my own gas. Also, thanks for coming to the party. I hope you had a nice time.

I enjoyed visiting with you at my graduation party. I'm sorry that your kids were not able to make it, but liked hearing the updates on all of them. Thanks for the crock pot. It will be very useful in my dorm room.

Thank you for the toaster. I will use it often in my dorm room as I love to warm up Pop-Tarts. Perhaps, I will also find a healthy alternative to toast. Thank you for coming to the party as well!

I was sorry to hear that you were not well enough to come to my graduation party. I hope you are feeling better now. Thank you for mailing the check. I am saving all graduation money for college expenses. I hear books can be expensive! I will stop by and visit with you before I head to [School Name].

Thank you for the graduation money. You are very generous! I will be putting it towards a used car this summer as I have a job now at [Company]. *I feel one step closer to being independent.*

I am grateful for [Book Title] *that you gave to me for graduation. I've started reading it already and it offers advice I can take action on right away to be better at managing my finances. Perhaps, we can get together in a few weeks to discuss. I would love to hear your thoughts on it. This could be a life changing book!*

I was excited to see you at my graduation party. Thank you so much for coming. I was very surprised. I hope you enjoyed the food and the cake. I also am grateful for the money you gave me. I will be spending it on new clothes for school, as I will need much warmer clothing when I move to [City/Region Name].

Thank you for the graduation gift. I will use the money towards items I discover I need once I move into the dorm. I am excited to start the next phase of my life.

You are very generous! Thank you for giving me so much. I was very surprised and will be diligent with how I spend the money. You can have confidence that I will use it only towards college expenses as indicated in your note. Thank you again for helping me to start college life.

COLLEGE

Graduating from college was one of the happiest days of my life. I felt very accomplished to receive a bachelor's degree. (I majored in math if you were wondering). I didn't have a big party for college graduation like I did for high school graduation, but I probably received a few gifts from family members—to be honest, I don't really remember!

For college graduation gifts people are probably more likely to give you money. You may find the chapter on how to write a thank you for money helpful as well. Beyond gifts, you can use this opportunity to thank the people that have supported you through college in ways that were not financial, such as mentoring and encouragement.

Examples:

Thank you for sending a card and check to recognize my graduation. I am excited to start interviewing for relevant jobs. I appreciate your support and will be putting the money towards a car that I can use once I have secured a position.

Thank you for the graduation money. I will be using it towards travel expenses. I am planning to move to [City Name] *now that I have a degree as they have many companies that specialize in* [Degree Field]. *There should be many opportunities for my career there.*

I am grateful for all the support you've given me while I've been studying the past four years. You believed in me and my abilities when I didn't. Thank you for encouraging me to keep learning and to stick with it. I love [Degree Field] *more than ever and look forward to my first job.*

Thank you for the money and card you mailed last week. I will use it for things I need as I start interviewing, including a nice suit. I am excited to be moving on with the next stage of my life.

I am extremely excited to have my degree! I want to thank you for meeting with me once each semester. I enjoyed hearing about what is happening in [Degree Field] *at your workplace. Your stories have inspired me that I can make a difference. I also thank you in advance for agreeing to be a reference once I land a job interview.*

Thank you for doing the independent study class with me during the summer. Because of it, I was able to graduate at the end of the summer instead of at the end of the fall semester. I enjoyed the book we read and then discussed together. It's given me a new outlook on [Topic].

I appreciate the money you sent to recognize my college graduation. And thank you for noting in the card that it's fine to spend it on something fun! I will use it to take my girlfriend and me out for a celebration dinner. We love the fancy sushi restaurant downtown and normally do not have the budget to go there. It will be a real treat.

I am looking forward to reading the book, [Name of Book]. Now that I've graduated it will give me new insights on [Topic]. I am excited that we share an interest in [Topic] and will follow up in a few months to let you know how the book as influenced me.

Thank you for the graduation card and encouraging note. Sharing your experience of how your degree impacted your life was inspiring to read. I appreciate the time you spent to write it out. Next time you are in town, let's plan to meet for lunch. I'd love to hear more details from your life story.

Thank you for supporting me during the past few years while I was in college. I am extremely excited to be finished! Your encouragement has meant a lot to me and I hope to pay it forward someday.

WEDDING

MOST COUPLES RECEIVE MANY GIFTS when they get married. The amount of gifts can easily be the most they've ever received at one time. While gifts for weddings can feel expected, keep in mind that while wedding gifts are very common when getting married, the giver still had to make a choice to give you a gift or not. Following up with a thank-you note will show your appreciation. For wedding gifts, I strongly recommend handwriting the thank-you notes.

Tips:

- **Be organized when opening your gifts.** Make a list of who gave you each gift. Download the free gift list tracker at www.tonsofthanks.com/resources. I've been married for thirteen years and still do not know who gave us the mini-crockpot due to my disorganization.

- **Keep your address list from when you wrote out the invitations.** This should help make it easier to address the thank-you note envelopes.

- **Do not try to write all the notes at one time if you have a lot** (more than ten) to write. Try to get them all done within one week. Some families may notice if one person got a thank you and the other didn't.

- **Be specific in your note and name the gift.** Otherwise, people will think you do not know what you gave to them. If you don't remember, write a note thanking them for the "gift." That is better than no note at all.

- **For money gifts, you do not need to mention the amount of the gift.**

- **Write the notes as soon as you can after the wedding and honeymoon.** It's better to write them and get them done than to let the task linger for months.

- **Don't procrastinate.** If you do not write the notes promptly, some people will begin to think you are lazy or ungrateful—or both!

- **Decide to make it fun.** Pick out cute thank-you cards, or make a custom card using a photo from the wedding. You can also order thank-you note cards that match your invitations.

- **Thank them for coming to the wedding, if they came to the wedding ceremony.**

- **If a person came to the wedding but did not give a gift, you do not need to thank them for coming with a note.** However, you can if you want to, or you may want to if they came a considerable distance to attend. Either way, if you know a gift was not in their budget, you can still recognize that they shared your wedding day with you if you'd like.

- **Both husband and wife can write the notes.** Regardless of who writes the note, the writer can sign both names.

Examples:

> Thank you for coming to our wedding. Also, we appreciate the crystal vase. Fresh flowers will look beautiful in it.

> We were surprised to get the gift card to the pet store! We will enjoy using it towards a new climbing tower for the cats. We love that you also love cats. Thanks for sharing our big day with us!

> We were delighted that you were able to come to the wedding. Thank you for your generous gift. We will use it towards a new couch. We will have you over for a visit once we have it.

> We were very happy to see you at the wedding! We appreciate the distance you traveled to attend. The new cookware will be put to good use. Thank You!

> Thank you for attending our wedding. We enjoyed visiting with you at the reception. We are looking forward to reading the Dave Ramsey book and learning how to get our finances in order.

> The picture frame is beautiful. Thank you for sending it. We are sorry to hear that you are unable to make it to the wedding. Our wedding photo is going to look great in that frame!

> The steak knives that you gave us for our wedding are wonderful. We love to grill steak on the weekends. We will have you over for steak this summer! Thank you for coming to the wedding.

> Thank you for the big crock pot! We are looking forward to making whole chickens and other recipes in it. Also,

thanks for coming to the wedding. We enjoyed catching up with you at the reception.

We received the check you mailed for our wedding. Thank you for being so generous! We will be saving it towards the down payment on our first house. We missed you at the wedding.

Thank you for being at the wedding! We've appreciated the support you've given us during the past few years. We have learned a lot from you about life and how to handle money wisely. Thank you for the wonderful set of dishes. They are beautiful and match our kitchen.

BABY SHOWER

CONGRATULATIONS ON YOUR BABY (or babies, if you are having twins or more at one time). Baby showers are a blessing in that your friends and family can help provide baby stuff.

Baby showers can be quite fun with the games, food, and opening of the gifts. Staying organized when opening the gifts will help you when writing the thank-you notes.

Tips:

- **Track your gifts.** While you open the gifts, a friend can record each gift and whom it was from.

- **Better safe than sorry.** If your shower is smaller (less than ten gifts expected), then you will likely remember what people gave to you. Or to be safe, make a list—just in case baby comes early. Then you will have a list to refer to later on when you have time to write the notes.

- **Try to write the notes before the baby or babies arrive.** If that didn't happen, it's okay if you take a while (months) to send out the thank-you notes. People generally understand that parents are very busy and tired with new babies.

- **Purchase thank-you notes before the baby shower.** If your shower is close to your baby's due date, plan to write them in the week following the baby shower to increase the likelihood of having them written before baby comes.

- **Do the work.** I do not recommend asking people to address their own thank-you note envelope at the shower. It can feel awkward to get something in the mail addressed in your own handwriting. Also, some people (not all) will think you are lazy if you decide to go this route. However, if the only way you will follow through with the thank-you notes is to have guests address their own envelope, go ahead and do it.

- **In addition to thanking people for the gifts, remember to thank the organizer, hostess and people who brought food.** Organizing an event like this can be time consuming!

- **Don't forget Dad!** If the father has a diaper party, he should write thank-you notes to everyone that brought diapers to the party!

Examples:

Thank you for the cloth diapers. I am excited to give them a try with the third baby. I enjoyed seeing you at the shower.

The cupcakes you brought to the shower were amazing! Thank you for taking the time to make them from scratch. They taste so much better that way. I also appreciate the warm jacket and slippers for the baby.

The shower was fun! Those were some creative games you came up with. Thank you for hosting the baby shower at your home. I had a nice time seeing the family. And I love the outfit for the baby.

Thank you for all of the baby supplies! The diaper "cake" was a fun game and also made for a fun way to give diapers. The lotions and wipes are also appreciated.

I am excited to try out the glass bottles. Another first for me with this baby. Thanks for coming to the shower!

Thank you for hosting and providing all of the food for my baby shower. I enjoyed the cake and nachos. I had a wonderful time visiting and playing games. Thank you also for the cloth diapers and outfits.

The homemade blanket for the baby is beautiful! The colors of it match the baby's room too. And the yarn is so soft! This was the perfect gift!

Thank you for coming to the baby shower and also for the cute outfits. The cat pictures on them are adorable. I hope the baby and my cats get along okay!

I am so excited that our babies are due around the same time. Thank you for the receiving blankets. They are so soft and the designs match the color of the baby's room.

Thank you for the gift card to [Store Name]. *I will use it towards items that I do not receive at the baby shower. I am sorry that you are not able to make it to the shower. I will send you some pictures soon.*

AFTER A FUNERAL

AFTER A FUNERAL, you may want to send out thank-you notes for flowers, food, donations, fruit baskets, or other gifts. Please know that you have my sympathy if you are in this situation.

Losing a loved one is difficult. If you are not up to writing thank-you notes, it's okay to delay writing them for a few weeks or even longer. Another idea is to have a friend or other family members help write the notes. When a parent passes away, divide the thank-you notes up between the siblings (or perhaps older grandchildren can help). When you are ready, the examples below can help you get started with your notes.

Q&A:

Should I write a thank-you note to those that came to the funeral but did not give a gift or donation? No. It's not necessary to thank those that were at the service or calling hours but did not give flowers or any other type of gift. If you want to, you can, but it's not expected.

Should I send a thank-you note for every sympathy card? No. Cards do not need to be acknowledged. You may want to respond with a thank you when a personal note was written in the card.

Tips:

- **Find your cards.** The funeral home may have printed cards with a verse on the inside that can be purchased. Then a personalized note can be included on the blank side. You can also order thank-you note cards of your choosing that are blank on the inside. Ordering through the funeral home will be likely be the easiest way to go.

- **Acknowledge all donations.** Sometimes donations can be made to an organization in lieu of flowers. The organization could be Hospice or the local Humane Society or a church, etc. It will be whatever the deceased requested. The donations are usually dropped off at the funeral home. The funeral home may provide you with the list or you may have to sort through the donations yourself. Also, if donations were made elsewhere, they may only provide you with a list if you request it.

- **The notes do not need to be long.** The goal is to acknowledge the gift, food, sympathy, etc.

- **Notes should be handwritten when possible.**

Examples:

FOR A DONATION

Thank you for making a donation to Hospice in memory of [Name of Deceased]. *We were grateful for the support of Hospice near the end of her life. Also, thank you for coming to the funeral.* [Name of Deceased] *shared many stories about you with the family in recent weeks.*

We appreciate your donation to the Humane Society made in honor of Uncle Joe. Joe was a dog lover his whole life and he would be happy knowing that more dogs will be helped.

FOR FLOWERS

The flowers for Betty's funeral were beautiful. The arrangement of purple carnations and white lilies was stunning and Betty would have loved them. Thank you for your kindness and remembering the family.

We appreciated the roses at my grandma's funeral. Roses were her favorite. Roses will always remind me of grandma.

FOR FOOD

Note: This could be for food brought to the funeral home for calling hours, or the after funeral meal, or food brought to your home before/after the funeral.

Thank you for organizing the food for the calling hours. The church has been a true blessing to us during this difficult time. The family loved the chicken wings and side dishes.

I was feeling completely overwhelmed when [Name of Deceased] *passed away. I appreciate the casseroles you brought over. I lived on them for a couple of weeks and may not have eaten otherwise. Thanks for being there for me.*

The after funeral meal at the church was wonderful. Thank you for hosting the family and providing all the food. Food is such a comfort in times like this. We were able to share many memories of [Name of Deceased] *during the meal.*

We were impressed with the meal following the funeral. The amount of food was perfect and the food tasted great. We also liked that there were gluten-free options without our specifically requesting it. Please pass on our thanks to the ladies who organized and prepared the meal.

TO THE FUNERAL DIRECTOR

When my mother-in-law died unexpectedly, we relied on the funeral director. He helped us with death certificates, cremation process, transportation of the deceased, and filing the obituary with the local newspaper. And that is just a small list of what funeral directors can do. Expressing your appreciation for their assistance is important, even in a difficult time.

Tips:

- **It's okay if you don't know what to say.** Browse funeral home websites that share thank-you notes as testimonials. If you do look at the site for the funeral home you use, just be sure that you do not exactly copy someone's note and then give it to them. It's very possible that they would recognize it as being from their own website!

- **Be inclusive.** If you worked with several people, it's fine to address the note to the staff of the funeral home.

Examples:

Thank you for helping us through the process from beginning to end. We were not prepared for mom's death. We appreciate all the support from the entire staff.

Having food delivered during the long day of calling hours was a fantastic idea. The family was thankful to be able to step away for a bite to eat while taking a break.

Thank you for insuring all the details of my Aunt [Name] funeral went smoothly. When she asked me to be her representative upon her passing, I was not sure what all that would entail. I was glad for your help with the obituary and obtaining the death certificates.

I want to thank you for all the time you spent with my family. Explaining each step helped us make decisions and feel in control of a very hard situation. Thank you for arranging for [Name of Deceased] to be taken to the church. Having the funeral at the church she attended for over 100 years was important to the family. Your suggestion to make a DVD with photos worked out very well as family and friends enjoyed viewing it during the calling hours.

Thank you for everything you and your staff did for [Name of Deceased] funeral. The room was the perfect size for the funeral and the organist did a great job playing the hymns. Everything went as well as possible given the situation. I appreciate that you were able to organize the pallbearers as that part was too stressful for me to deal with at the time.

We appreciate the kindness of all of the staff during the calling hours and funeral for my grandma. She was a special lady and I am thankful that everything went smoothly. The family appreciated the snacks that were on hand for the calling hours too.

People

SPOUSE

THANKING YOUR SPOUSE with a thank-you note is a great way to show your appreciation for everything that they do. Getting handwritten thanks and recognition from you will likely be a very nice surprise! They also have the potential to improve your relationship.

Tips:

- **Include specific examples of what you appreciate about him/her.** "Thank you for all you do, you are great" feels like a printed message in a greeting card. Use your own words to let them know what you are grateful for.

- **Show gratitude for thoughtful acts.** My husband helps with the dishes and cleaning up the kitchen. Sometimes he will make the meal. What has your spouse done recently that you would like to recognize? Think about this and then include those things in the note. Have they helped extra with the kids? Did they take care of you and the household when you were sick? Are they working hard every day so that you can be a stay at home parent? Did they work overtime to earn extra money to buy you something special?

Thanking your spouse will likely be a more personal note than a typical thank-you note. The examples below are based on my own experiences and imagination. They should help you get started if you are not sure what to say. Remember to personalize it. The notes can be concluded with "Love" or "I Love You," followed by your name.

Examples:

Thank you for consistently helping with the dishes. As you know, I love to cook but not clean up afterward. I am grateful for you taking on this task as it keeps me motivated to make healthy meals for us.

I appreciate your help last week with the kids. I needed the break! My energy has returned and I look forward to returning to the regular routine. The kids and I are thankful for how hard you work so that I can stay at home with them.

I was surprised when you started working overtime. I am thankful that you did! The new furniture is exactly what I wanted. It's perfect for the room and we can enjoy it together while watching our favorite shows.

I want to let you know how thankful I am that you agreed to read The Total Money Makeover and follow the advice. Our finances and marriage are stronger because of it. I am looking forward to us becoming debt-free!

I love being married to you! I had so much fun with you on the picnic and hike last weekend. Thank you for organizing it. It was the perfect surprise and the day together was just what we needed.

Thank you for taking such good care of me while I was sick last week. I appreciate that you made me soup and brought it to me on the couch. (And thank you for washing the blankets after I spilled soup on them.)

Happy Anniversary! Thank you for all of the flowers and cards you've given me each year. They make me feel loved and appreciated.

I love that we have learned to compromise. Thank you for agreeing to let me keep two kittens. They are super-cute and I've become quite attached. They will be snuggling with you soon!

Thank you for all of your support as I work to get my side business going. It is taking much longer than I expected to make a profit. Your unwavering support has helped me to keep going. I love you very much and hope to show you a profit soon.

Last week was rough for me! I didn't expect to have long-lasting pain after my teeth were removed. I am thankful that you took such good care of me and made soft food that I could eat. I'm glad this experience is behind us— but you can cook for me anytime!

TEACHER

Teachers spend countless hours helping your child learn and grow. Why not show your appreciation to one of the biggest influences in your child's life?

The teacher will appreciate hearing that they are doing a good job. A little gratitude can go a long way in encouraging teachers that their efforts are worth it!

HOW TO SHOW YOUR APPRECIATION TO A TEACHER:

- **A handwritten thank-you note or letter**
- **An emailed thank-you note or letter**
- **A "thank you" in person**
- **A small trinket for their desk**
- **A gift card (Starbucks, Amazon, local restaurants, etc.)**
- **Invite them to the high school graduation party for your student**
- **Invite them to your college graduation party**

A combination of these methods can be used. For example, you can send a note with a small gift. The thank-you can come from a parent or the student.

Also, the teacher may not have a preference of how they are thanked. If you know a certain teacher loves thank-you notes, then send them a handwritten thank you.

Do not get hung up on the method. If you don't want to handwrite a thank-you note, then please email them or tell them in person! The point here is that the teacher is getting thanked one way or another.

NOTE: Gifts are nice and perhaps easier to do than writing a thank-you note or coming up with the words to say in person. Some teachers are much more likely to remember your words than what gift you gave them. A teacher once told me:

"Coming down to my mailbox and finding a stack of notes inside is always heart-warming and makes me feel I made the right decision to become a teacher."

YOU CAN THANK A TEACHER FOR...

- **Doing a great job.** Your child has taken an interest in a subject because of how well the teacher is teaching it.

- **Inspiring your child.** Does your child want to be a teacher because of a specific teacher? I'd say that means the teacher is having an impact and should be thanked!

- **Showing your child a great time.** Your child went on a class trip and they can't stop talking about it.

- **Improving your child's grades or scores.** The teacher helped your child learn how to study for a test. As a result, the students test scores are improving.

- **Improving your child's behavior.** Has your child's behavior improved as a result of the teacher's efforts?

- **Making learning fun.** Did the teacher do a fun experiment or game in classroom exercise that helped your student learn the subject matter?

Tips:

- **Stay formal.** If the note is coming from the student, do not use the teacher's first name. Use Mr., Mrs. or Ms. or however they refer to the teacher at school.

- **Use the note as a genuine way to thank the teacher.** Resist the urge to "suck up" to the teacher.

- **Thank the teacher as situations occur instead of waiting for Christmas or end of the year.** Teachers like encouragement all year long!

- **The note does not need to be a novel.** Three or Four sentences will do! If you have a lot to say, a longer note is fine too.

Examples:

FROM THE PARENT

[Student's Name] *is really enjoying your class this year!* [He/She] *is excited about all the interactive projects you do with the class. Your efforts are appreciated!* [Student's Name] *is learning more about* [Subject] *than ever before!*

Thank you for teaching [Student's Name] *how to study for a test. She has been a weak test taker for years and I haven't been able to find a way to help her. Your method is working. Her test scores have improved in not only your class, but all other classes as well. The time you have spent with her will make a long term difference in her life.*

You have been a huge blessing to my family. Because of the extra time you have spent teaching [Student's Name] *the "new" way of doing math, the stress in my household has reduced considerably. My husband and I still want to do it the "old" way that we learned in school. We are very thankful that* [Student's Name] *now fully grasps the concepts and can do his homework on his own.*

Thank you for making [Class Subject] *interesting!* [Student Name] *is enjoying your class so much that he does his homework on his own and is excited to share with us what he is learning. He also wants us to visit the museum that you took the class too. This is the most excited he has ever been to go to school. He loves your class! You are an excellent teacher!*

The turnaround in [Student's Name]*'s attitude has been amazing this year.* [He/She] *talks about your class often and shares what* [he/she] *is learning. We also no longer have to fight with* [her/him] *to do his homework for any class. Whatever you are doing works!* [He/She] *loves to learn new things now.*

FROM THE STUDENT

Thank you for helping me with my math assignments. The way you've been able to explain things to me after class has helped me a lot. I am finally understanding algebra!

I loved being in your class this year. The way you teach makes [Class Subject] *fun and interesting to learn about. I wish you could be my teacher for every class!*

Thank you for being my teacher. I had fun and learned a lot. You are the best. (Note: this short example is for a younger student.)

Thank you for all the support you've given me throughout high school. You are an excellent teacher and I will be going on to study [Subject Name] *at college because of you. Will you please attend my high school graduation party?* [Include party invitation in envelope.]

I have been inspired by your class to learn more about [Subject]. *Thank you for making the topic interesting. I feel that your class has changed my life and how I think about* [Subject]. *I will be using the knowledge from your class to help make the lives of others better.*

AUTHOR

AUTHORS SPEND MANY HOURS writing books each year. What can you do to let an author know that their book is appreciated? When a book impacts your life in a significant way, I recommend sending them a thank-you. This can be done with a handwritten note, in an email, on Facebook, Twitter, or other social media sites.

Tips:

- **Buy their book.** Buying the book will generate revenue for them and, on sites like Amazon, it will increase their sales ranking. (Thank you for buying this book!)

- **Write a review.** This could be on Amazon, another online store or on your website. When I see many positive reviews, I am much more likely to make the purchase.

- **Tell others about the book.** This can be done in several ways. I track the books I am reading on Goodreads. My Goodreads friends can see all of the books I have read. Perhaps they will see something on my list and want to read it too.

- **Share the book.** Another way to tell others is by sharing what you are reading on your website (if you have one). Or, if appropriate, you could interview the author to introduce them to your audience.

- **Talk about the book on social media.** Links to the books can also be shared on social media. For example, on Facebook, you could write a summary of why you liked the book or why you think others should read it and include an Amazon link to the book.

- **Read it for book club.** Several of the books I've read this year were selections for my church book club or the book club at work. One of the great things about book clubs is it exposes us to authors we may not have read otherwise.

Template:

NOTE: Many authors have a website. Look for their mailing address or email address on their site.

Dave Ramsey's book, *The Total Money Makeover*, helped my family get on a budget and out of debt. This was several years ago. I sent him a thank-you note similar to this one:

> *Dear Dave,*
>
> *I want to let you know that your book, The Total Money Makeover, has helped my family get on a budget. We were also able to pay off all of our debts except for the mortgage. I felt like I got a raise once I knew where all my money was going each month. Thank you for writing the book and sharing your story to help others.*
>
> *Thanks again,*
>
> *Heidi*

Examples:

> *Thank you for writing* [Book Title]. *I found myself laughing all the way through it. The book was very enjoyable to read and I could relate well to* [Character Name].

> *The tips in your book have helped me become more productive! Before your book, I was wasting so much time figuring out what to do and how to spend my time on my projects. Thank you for your instructions on how to be organized and stay on schedule. I will be recommending your book often!*

> *Your book,* [Book Title], *was very intriguing. Everyone in my book club enjoyed reading it. Only one of us had figured out who the murderer was before the end of book. I am looking forward to reading your next exciting book!*

> *Thank you for signing my copy of your book at your book signing at* [Location]. *Having an autographed copy of one of my all-time favorite books is wonderful. I enjoyed every page of the book and will be giving away several as gifts! You are very inspiring.*

> *Your book,* [Book Title], *was one of the best I've ever read. Thank you for writing it. I can relate to the story and will be sharing it with my friends. I got so much enjoyment out of it. I hope you plan to add more books to this series!*

> *I enjoyed reading* [Book Title]. *While the book was fictional, I was inspired by the story to make some changes in my own life regarding* [Topic]. *The way* [Main Character] *changed over time was more helpful for me to read than a typical how-to book on the subject. Thank you for sharing this story.*

I am excited to share [Book Title] *with everyone who will listen! The information on* [Topic] *is explained well for the casual reader. I am already seeing the benefits from implementing your tips on* [subject]. *Thank you for sharing your ideas through the book.*

I love the cats in the cat coloring book that you designed. Some of them remind me of my cats. It has been a joy to color them. On rough days the coloring has calmed my soul. I will be ordering another after I color every page.

Thank you for your words of wisdom in [Book Title]. *Sometimes I need to hear advice about* [Topic] *from someone that I am not related to or know in real life. The examples you shared on how to change* [Habit] *seem like they will work for me. I am going to try them and see if anyone notices.*

Thank you for writing the series of books about the [Name] *family. This note is a little overdue since you are currently working on book 18. I've grown to love and know the family like they are my own. I have learned from their ups and downs. I've cried with them and laughed with them. I wanted you to know how much I've enjoyed the books over the years and I hope to meet you some day at a book signing.*

GUEST POST HOST

A GUEST POST IS WRITING you share on someone else's blog or website that provides value to their readers. The owner of the blog or website is the guest post host. Guest posting is usually done as a marketing strategy.

The first guest post I did was on Jon Stolpe's Stretched blog. It was an article on how to encourage children to write thank-you notes. The guest post (hopefully) brought value to his readers, and helped me reach new people. I mailed him a thank-you note shortly after to thank him for the opportunity.

After your post goes live on another person's site, take a few minutes to thank the host. This may or may not be your first time interacting with the host. A thank-you will leave a great impression.

HOW TO SHOW YOUR
APPRECIATION TO A GUEST POST HOST:

- **A handwritten thank-you note**

- **An email thank-you note**

- **A small gift**

- **A public thank-you on social media**

A combination of the above can be used as well.

I would only recommend sending a gift if you know the host well enough to know what type of gift they will appreciate. Perhaps, they have mentioned their favorite type of coffee or they are a chocolate lover.

Another option is to send a thank-you email the day your post goes live and then send a handwritten note in the mail a few days later. If you wait a few days, then you can let the guest post host know the impact the guest post had on your site.

YOU CAN THANK A GUEST POST HOST FOR...

- **Their Time.** The host most likely spent time reading and possibly making edits to your article before posting. Then there is the technical time to get it posted to the site. They may also have spent time promoting the post on social media.

- **Access to their audience.** A guest post on another's site is a great way to introduce yourself and your site to new readers.

Examples:

> *Thank you for allowing me to share my message with your audience. Over 1,000 people have visited my site after reading the guest post, and many have signed up for my newsletter.*

> *I am thankful for the opportunity to share a post on your site! I appreciate the time you spent reviewing the article and suggesting edits to improve it. If you ever want to post on my site, let me know!*

My guest post on your site boosted views on my site by 50% during the past three days. I thank you for giving me the opportunity to share my message with your audience. By the number of comments on the post, I think they found the information valuable. I also am grateful for your editing skills and improving the article. I have learned a lot from you during this process.

I had fun guest posting on your site! The comments and interaction were great. Thank you for having me on your site to talk about [Topic]. *I also appreciate your time in getting it set up and helping with revisions.*

Thank you for having me do a guest post on your site. I also appreciate how often you shared the link to it on social media. It seems that talking about [Topic] *was a success as many people decided to visit my site after reading the article. I've gained several hundred email subscribers!*

Wow! I had no idea how successful a guest post could be. Thank you so much for inviting me to share the article about [Topic] *with your audience. Several people have since reached out to me asking for me to share an article with their audience. You were right about the networking possibilities!*

Thank you for reaching out to me to do a guest post on your site. I think it was a huge success for both of us, based on how many people viewed the article from my social media sites. Also, thank you for having your assistant help with the editing and getting just the right picture.

Thank you for teaching me the ins and outs of guest posting by having me post an article on your blog. I understand the process much better now which will help me when I reach out to other bloggers or when someone asks to share an article on my site. I am glad that my article was received so well by your readers.

I want to tell you again how grateful I am for being able to guest post for you. As a new blogger, it has been tough getting my name out there. The guest post has boosted my credibility and I've had an increase in traffic and email sign-ups. Thank you for giving me the opportunity and for all the time you spent reading drafts of the post!

Thank you for reaching out to me to guest post on your site. I had a great time interacting with your audience. And I noticed that you promoted the article on your social media accounts. This helped me to gain several "likes" and "followers" that are very interested in [Topic]. *Please let me know if you'd like to do a guest post on my site.*

SOCIAL MEDIA

On social media, you need to remember to tag the person in the post so that they get a notification that you are thanking them. On Twitter and Instagram this is done by using the @ sign before the person's handle. For the examples, I will use *@HeidiABender*, which is my Twitter handle. To increase visibility of the tweet, place their twitter handle at the middle or end of the tweet. You can also share the link to the post. Instagram does not limit the amount of text that can be shared. Twitter limits posts to 140 characters.

Thanks for having me as a guest poster on your site today, @HeidiABender. [Insert link to post.]

Hey @HeidiABender, *thanks for having me on your blog today!* [Insert link to post.]

I am honored to be posting on @HeidiABender site! Read this post about [Subject] *here* [Insert link to post.]

VIRTUAL ASSISTANT

Vɪʀᴛᴜᴀʟ Aѕѕɪѕᴛᴀɴᴛѕ ᴄᴀɴ ᴅᴏ ʜᴜɴᴅʀᴇᴅѕ of tasks for you. Is your Virtual Assistant saving you time and therefore money? Are they awesome? Have you told them lately?

One goal of having a virtual assistant is to save time. They can do things that you either do not want to do, do not know how to do, or prefer not to do. Writing your virtual assistant a thank-you note occasionally is one way to praise them. Your virtual assistant may also like a gift, but we will stick to thank-you notes in this chapter.

The thank-you notes should thank them for something specific. "Thanks for the help" is too generic to be meaningful. I also recommend sending handwritten notes sometimes as the person can display them on their desk or bulletin board as a visual reminder of your gratitude.

Examples:

> *Thank you for researching* [Topic] *for me. The way you compiled the lists and organized the information made it very easy for me to write the blog post about* [Topic]. *The post was a huge success!*

I want to take a moment to let you know how much I appreciate your transcribing skills. Your accuracy for transcribing the podcasts is exceptional. We have received several emails thanking us for providing them and having the technical words spelled correctly has helped with our site SEO. I will be recommending you to [Name] *who is in search of transcription services.*

Wow! I looked at the photos in Dropbox today, and I'm impressed with how well you have them organized. I will be able to find what I need much faster with the tags you've added. I used to spend hours looking for pictures on specific topics. I thank you for your patience with sorting through all of them!

Your social media sharing skills are excellent! I noticed a significant increase in shares, likes, and clicks since you've taken over posting to social media sites. I am amazed at your results. The Pinterest boards are much more organized now and are helping people find more information on topics they are interested in. Awesome work!

I logged into [Email Service] *today and noticed how well the lists are organized. This is not something I could have quickly accomplished on my own. I greatly appreciate your help with managing the lists. We will be able to serve the newsletter subscribers much better now.*

I am very happy with your graphic design work. The new logo and all that goes along with it (banners, etc.) look great. We have also received many compliments from readers. Having you on board for the graphics is wonderful and saves me so much time as I struggled with the design work. The site looks professional now!

Thank you for maintaining the WordPress plugins and themes. The way you have been able to customize the theme has improved the customer experience on the site. Visitors are staying on the site 50% longer with your design improvements! I am looking forward to seeing the next round of improvements. And I can take comfort knowing that all plugins are being updated as soon as new versions are released.

The landing pages you have created are wonderful! I thought I was good at them until you showed me what you can do! Enrollment in [Course Name] *is up 20% just by the changes you made. I am thankful for your A/B testing abilities. The results are literally paying for the time to complete the testing.*

Thank you for finding great places for my family and me to go to when we visit [Travel Destination]. *I appreciate the hours of research you did. I am looking forward to the restaurants as well. The seafood place right on the beach sounds amazing. Thank you for taking the stress out of the trip by organizing it for us!*

I want to let you know how much I appreciate the time you spent on [Project Name]. *The results are much better than I anticipated. The graphics you designed are perfect for the landing page. I am excited for future projects as this one is going so well!*

DENTIST

THE DENTIST IS SOMETIMES FEARED or even hated. Remember that "the dentist" is a real person with real feelings! You may not like the pain associated with some dental visits, but you can still like and appreciate your dentist! National Dentist's Day is celebrated every year on March 6th. I am sure your dentist would appreciate a "thank-you" anytime of the year!

I recommend sending a handwritten note to the dentist after a successful procedure or other experience. Their office mailing address is probably going to be easier to find than their email address. And a handwritten thank-you note can be put on display. If the office chooses, they may also use your note as a testimonial on the website for their office (hopefully, they will ask your permission first).

Examples:

> *Thank you for the wonderful work on the fillings on my front teeth. The shade of white you used perfectly matches my other teeth. The filling is not noticeable at all. Also, the office staff is very nice and helpful whenever I schedule appointments or having billing questions.*

> *As you know, I had a bit of anxiety before getting my first crown. Thank you for taking the time to answer*

all my questions about the procedure beforehand. This helped me feel more comfortable with the procedure. I am very happy with the result. The crown looks great!

I was impressed with your kindness and patience when I learned the bad news about my teeth. It was hard for me to hear that the two of them needed to be pulled! Thank you for going over the X-rays in detail and explaining the problem. I also appreciate how quickly you were able to connect me with the dental specialist.

My teeth look fantastic! I am very grateful for the whitening process that you recommended. After only [Duration], I am getting compliments how great my teeth look. My confidence in public is growing every day. Thank you for being a great dentist!

My kids love having you as their dentist. All fears they had of "going to the dentist" have been removed. [Name] was scared when he found out that he needed a filling. Afterward, he said it wasn't so bad and you are a nice guy!

Thank you for pulling out my bad tooth during the middle if the night. I am grateful that you respond to emergency calls. The pain was more than I could bear. I am very thankful to have that tooth out and will be more diligent with self-dental care going forward.

I appreciate the extra time you have spent adjusting my bite at no charge! Thank you for being patient and making multiple adjustments as I get used to wearing this bite split. I am already feeling an improvement in the jaw pain!

I want to thank you for your wonderful bedside manner. Your explanations about the [Procedure] helped me to relax. I will be recommending you to all of my friends!

DOCTOR

MY LIFE WAS SAVED BY A DOCTOR when I was born six weeks early. My twin brother and I were born in the early morning hour and he arrived first. Somewhere along the way, the nurses recognized that the on-call doctor was making poor choices regarding the delivery. My mother's regular baby doctor arrived and saved my life! I was born breech, 34 minutes after my brother. I was only given 20% chance of surviving. If the regular doctor had not come in, I might not be here today writing this for you!

Whatever the reason, if you are feeling grateful to your doctor, take a few minutes to thank him or her. Doctors can feel intimidating because of their title, but remember they are regular people. They studied for many years to earn the Doctor title. They still have feelings and like to be appreciated!

National Doctor's Day is celebrated on March 30th in the United States. This is a great time to thank your doctor for general care. For major events like having a baby, surgery, saving your life or other emergency, I recommend sending a thank-you note shortly thereafter (within a couple of weeks).

If you are not sure what to say in a thank-you note to

your doctor, these examples will help you to get started.

Tips:

- **Use their title.** I recommend starting the thank-you note with "Dear Dr. [Last Name]," unless you are on a first-name basis with your doctor.

- **Make sure he/she knows why you're thanking them.** There are hundreds of possible reasons to see a doctor. When you write a thank-you note to your doctor, be sure to include that reason.

Examples:

DELIVERING YOUR BABY

Thank you for delivering [Baby's Name] *and all the care leading up to the delivery. I have recovered well and appreciate all the advice and tips you gave me beforehand about how to deliver a baby. The class you recommend at* [Location] *was fantastic and helped me to feel less anxious about the process. I look forward to seeing you again when I become pregnant again.*

Delivering my latest baby was much easier than I anticipated. Thank you for coming to the hospital during the middle of the night to deliver [Baby's Name]. *I was very glad to have you there since you've been caring for me since the start of the pregnancy. Your easygoing manner helped me to relax. I am glad everything went so well!*

Thank you for recognizing that I needed to have an emergency C-section. From what the nurses told me, your quick decision and analysis of the situation likely saved my life and the baby's. We will always feel grateful towards you. [Baby's Name] *and I are both recovering well.*

SAVING YOUR LIFE

You are amazing! Thank you for saving my life. I'm so thankful that you noticed the abnormal blood result and ordered the ultrasound which clearly showed the blockage. The pain was immeasurable and I felt like I was not going to make it. As you later shared, I would not have made it much longer without having surgery.

I was so scared when I found out I had diabetes that I ignored it. I am grateful to your office staff for their consistent calls requesting that I have a checkup visit. If it weren't for their persistence, I might never have made an appointment. Thank you for checking my blood levels at that visit. As you know, I was nearly in a coma from the high sugar level. Having that test done saved my life!

Having surgery is scary, knowing that there is a risk that something can go wrong. I'm thankful for all you did to save me when things didn't go as expected. [You can include details of what went wrong, if you choose]. *I am here today because of your efforts. I will always be grateful for what you did.*

YOUR SURGEON

Thank you for your excellent work while performing surgery on me for [Condition]. *Your hands are skilled as my incision is very small and my pain has been minimal during recovery. I will be recommending you to everyone I know who also has* [Condition].

I am grateful for the surgery you did to remove my gall

bladder. I feel so much better now. Thank you for taking it out even though the tests did not indicate a major problem. The tests on it after it was removed confirmed it was making me sick!

I was very nervous about having surgery for [Condition]! *Thank you for describing what would happen before, during, and after the surgery. The information provided helped me to move forward with the surgery. I am feeling much better now and am thankful that there were not any complications during the surgery.*

YOUR GENERAL CARE PHYSICIAN

Thank you for your reliable care year after year. The guidance you have given me regarding exercise and nutrition at my annual physical has proved to keep me healthy. I am grateful for only needing to see you once a year.

I appreciate your help with my [Condition]. *Thank you for answering all my questions about it. More information helps me feel better about the medication that is prescribed and why I need to take it. I also enjoy your easy going manner and jokes!*

Thank you for squeezing in my daughter, [Child's Name], *last week for her annual physical. She needed it to participate in volleyball and of course, I forgot about it until the day before practices were to start. I am happy to report that she made the team!*

FINANCIAL ADVISOR

Has a financial advisor helped you with your finances in some way? Did they recommend an investment that has yielded a great return? Did they help you rollover your 401k when you changed jobs? My advisor has helped me enroll in a Roth IRA and answered all of my questions about it. He was a huge help!

I encourage you to write your financial advisor a thank-you note. This will show them your gratitude for how they have helped you. Especially since the services they provide are things you'd rather not figure out how to do on your own.

Examples:

>*Thank you for helping me enroll in a Roth IRA. I had been feeling overwhelmed with the process. I also appreciate that you did all the paperwork for monthly automatic withdrawals. I will be saving money without having to remember doing it.*

>*I am much more comfortable choosing funds for my investment portfolio after our discussion last week. I appreciate the extra time you spent answering my questions. I needed to understand the details before making the investment. I hope to see a great return soon!*

I was very pleased when I opened my statement this month. The funds you recommended are doing great this quarter! I am thankful that I trusted your advice. Let's plan to meet twice a year to review my portfolio.

Thank you for explaining the various forms of life insurance and how each one works. I am happy with my selection for a term policy. I also found the arrangement to have a nurse come to my home for the life insurance blood tests quite convenient. And thanks for doing all the paperwork!

Changing jobs was a very stressful time for me last month. I was very happy that you were able to transfer my 401k to an IRA for me. That saved me some time and stress. And I like the funds you choose in the IRA. I am grateful to be able to rely on you.

I received my quarterly statement from [Investment Company Name] *today. I am impressed with the returns in the funds you helped me choose. I am excited to see how much my money will grow by next quarter. Thank you for helping me get these investments set up.*

Thank you for handling my 401lk rollover! I was glad to trust you with it since I was busy packing to move to [State] *for the new job. I am pleased with the fund distribution and look forward to continuing to work with you.*

Thank you for helping me to get my savings in order. The automatic withdrawal for the Roth IRA was exactly what I needed to make saving easy. Now I don't have to think about it and will have a considerable amount saved in just a few years.

Thank you for explaining the various types of retirement accounts available. Meeting with me to explain it in person, was better for me than reading articles online. Thank you for being patient with all of my questions!

The meeting we had last week has changed my life! I am excited to start saving now that I understand how compound interest works. I will be recommending all of my college friends to you. The way you explained things made sense to me and I'm confident that you can help them as well.

ACCOUNTANT/BOOKKEEPER

ACCOUNTANTS AND BOOKKEEPERS both help manage finances but perform different functions. Sending your accountant or bookkeeper a gift or thank-you note will let them know how much you appreciate them!

Also, if they are working at a place with other accountants and bookkeepers, your gift has the potential to make them stand out to the boss. The boss may think they really helped out the customer as the customer appreciated it enough to send a gift. What a great compliment!

HOW TO SHOW YOUR APPRECIATION
TO YOUR ACCOUNTANT OR BOOKKEEPER:

- **Order pizza for them on or near Tax Day**, which is usually April 15 in the United States. This is their busy season, and they are often working long hours.

- **Send brownies, cookies or a fruit basket.** You may choose to bless the entire accounting department with a large basket that it can be shared.

- **Get "punny."** Accountants are often called "bean counters." If you know your accountant likes jellybeans, sending them some is a cute way of saying thanks as well.

- **Send a gift card to their favorite coffee place.**

- **Don't forget a note!** A handwritten thank-you note can be included with the gifts mentioned, or sent instead of a gift. They may appreciate your words more than a physical gift!

Examples:

> *Thank you for being diligent with the record keeping. I am very happy and relieved that you found the receipt I misplaced. I appreciate all the time you spend keeping the books balanced. It makes things go much smoother at tax time.*

> *I am very grateful for the extra time you spent running the financial reports this week. We were able to identify several areas where we can save costs because of your efforts. Your time was well spent.*

> *I am so excited to have you as my CPA! All the stress I had at tax time when I was doing the work myself is gone. You are a blessing. I am thankful to have you as part of my team.*

> *What a year it has been! You have done a wonderful job keeping track of all the receipts. I am grateful for how organized you are! I also appreciate your accuracy.*

> *I hope you like jelly beans! You are my favorite bean counter and I appreciate all that you do to keep the finances in order. I take comfort knowing that you are in*

charge of the books. I hope tax time goes well for you!

You have been a joy to work with as my bookkeeper. I am amazed at how quickly you are able to categorize the payments and run the weekly reports. Thank you for being awesome!

Thank you for another smooth tax season! I love that I can drop off all my stuff and a week later all I need to do is sign the form. You are worth every penny.

I am grateful that we can depend on you to keep the books straight. I appreciate how closely you pay attention to the details. Thank you for helping to correct the issue (that you also discovered) while reviewing the [Quarterly/Monthly] *data. I'm so glad that was resolved before taxes were due.*

Thank you for another great year of reliable service. I am glad we connected at that conference so many years ago. I am grateful for your understanding of the tax laws as I'm sure you've saved the company thousands over the years.

Thank you for being diligent with the monthly reporting. The reports you've designed are excellent and help me to understand the company's finances. They are a big improvement over scanning spreadsheets!

PERSONAL TRAINER

ARE YOU SEEING GREAT RESULTS after working with a personal trainer? Thank them. Let them know that their program worked for you!

In your note you can detail the results that you have experienced. The thank-you note may read like a testimonial. They may share it with others (hopefully, with your permission) on their website or display it on-site on a billboard. Thank-you notes indicate success!

Thank them for the results. Thank them for their time, or for the program if it is self-guided.

Tips:

- **Choose the easiest method of delivery.** If you are working 1:1 or in a small group in person with a trainer, then you could hand deliver the thank-you note. If you know your trainer well, you could also ask them for their address or mail it to their gym location. If that would feel weird, then ask for their email address if you would prefer to email the thank-you note.

- **Include the group.** If you are in an online group program, then you may be getting emails that contain their mailing address for handwritten thank-you notes. Or you can email them the note. If you only know them through an online program, I would NOT recommend asking them for their address if it is not in their email newsletter.

Examples:

Thank you for outlining an exercise program just for me. I am finally seeing results! My body feels great. I am very thankful for your personal support.

I have lost [Number of Pounds] *pounds since starting your program! I am so excited. I've had fun buying smaller sizes of clothing. I am telling all my friends about your program!*

I have seen great success going through [Program Name]. *I like that I can go at my own pace. I didn't take a "before" picture but can tell you that I've lost three inches from my waist so far! Your program is working for me. Thank you so much for sharing it online.*

What an adventure your class has been! I have lost weight, feel stronger, and I'm more confident than I have ever been before. This class has been life changing!

Thank you for introducing me to [Program Name]. *I am enjoying following the videos in my own at home. It's nice to not feel like anyone is judging (like can happen at the gym). My arms are starting to look fantastic!*

I appreciate the amount of time you've spent meeting with me at the gym. This type of exercise is all new to me. Thank you for answering all of my questions and demonstrating all of the moves for me. My body is already starting to feel stronger after the first few weeks.

I feel great in my new pants! I am amazed that I can fit into size [Number] *now. Your program has worked for me. Thank you for your support and accountability.*

I am enjoying working out with you 1:1. The individual attention is what I needed to reach my goals. I am also thankful for the easy to follow meal plan. I will be recommending you to my friends.

Thank you for encouraging me to exercise. I am surprised at how much I like lifting weights. The results are amazing! I am getting so many compliments on my arms.

I feel like the years are dropping off the more I get into shape while working with you. This is the best I have felt in my life. Thank you for helping me to feel better about myself and to finally get in shape. Your support is exactly what I needed.

FARMER

FARMERS ARE AWESOME. Farming ranks high on my list of admired profession as farmers provide most of the food we eat. And I like to eat! When I was younger, I also enjoyed visiting the farm of a family from my church. I loved the animals, the land, and even the smells!

October 12 is National Farmer's Day, also known as Old Farmer's Day. This is the perfect time of year to thank a farmer. If you personally know a farmer, I suggest thanking them with a thank-you note. If you visit a farmer's market, take a minute to say "thank you" to the farmer when making a purchase.

My husband and I met a farmer at our local farmer's market. We signed up for his delivery service. Once a week, we receive a delivery of chicken eggs and various meats (whatever we order). Recently, we also decided to order 1/2 a pig. This offers significant savings compared to purchasing by the pound each week. Here is the thank-you note that I wrote to him:

> *Thank you for your home delivery service. We love the*
> *fresh meats and eggs that come from your farm. We also*

appreciate that you wash the eggs for us. Also, thank you for explaining the pork cut sheet last week and always being willing to answer our questions.

Examples:

The non-GMO veggies we get from you are the best veggies we have ever had! Thank you for taking the extra time and effort to grow organic food. We are grateful to have a source of locally grown food!

We loved visiting your farm last week. The kids are still talking about it! Learning where food comes from and how it grows was a very educational experience. Thank you for answering all of their questions! We are looking forward to your next "learn about your food" day!

Thank you for raising grass feed cows! I like knowing that they get to graze and have great living conditions. Their meat also tastes delicious!

I am so glad to see you at the farmer's market each week. Your prices are great and your produce is wonderful. The kids also enjoy the homemade egg noodles! Thank you for keeping it local.

Thank you for being a farmer. I enjoy eating the food grown by you. It tastes so fresh and better than anything at the grocery store. Thank you for the service you provide to our community.

The tomatoes from your farm are the best I have ever had. We also appreciate that you do not use pesticides on them. I am convinced that organic tomatoes taste the best! Thank you for providing such delicious tomatoes.

We enjoyed the tour of your farm and seeing how the cows are cared for. Also, the milk is fantastic. We think it tastes better from the glass bottles and it's nice to know where the milk came from! We thank you for all of your efforts to set up and run a local dairy farm. It is wonderful for the entire community.

We love the produce you bring to the farmer's market. We are thankful to be able to eat local vegetables as they seem to taste better. And, thanks to your dedication to growing vegetables, we do not feel like we need a garden at home. You are our favorite farmer!

We were excited to discover your eggs! Also, thank you for showing us around the chickens and chicken coop. I love that you've given each chicken a name. Thank you for all the time and effort to raise and feed the chickens naturally. We feel their eggs are more nutritious this way.

Thank you for being a farmer and selling products at the farmer's market. The kids are also looking forward to your farm tours in the spring. We want them to know and appreciate where the food comes from! We will call to schedule an appointment in a few months.

PASTOR

Pastors only work one hour a week on Sundays...or so the joke goes.

Your pastor has many responsibilities and supports the congregation in many ways. They perform weddings, speak at funerals, prepare sermons, visit you when sick, provide prayer, and much more. Perhaps, the pastor preached a meaningful and maybe even life changing message.

Take a moment to thank him or her. Don't wait for Pastor Appreciation Day (the second Sunday in October) or Pastor Appreciation Month (all of October). Thank them throughout the year to let them know their efforts are appreciated.

I suggest thanking them with a thank-you note. You could also give a Starbucks gift card or other gift card if you know what they like. You can also consider ordering pizza for their family (just be sure to organize the date in advance).

Examples:

> *Thank you for performing our wedding ceremony. We were honored to have you as part of our big day. The short message was touching and everyone liked your jokes.*

I want to thank you for your message last Sunday. I will be taking action and making some changes in my life. I felt like your words were meant for me.

I appreciate the time you have spent counseling me this last month. Going through this unwanted divorce has been hard for me. Your words and prayers have been comforting.

Thank you for visiting me in the hospital after I had surgery. Your presence was a comfort. I appreciate the prayers. And thanks for bringing me some snacks!

Your messages in the current series on [Topic] have been excellent. I have been looking for ways to implement the ideas. Yesterday at work was a start when I told a friend about [Topic]. Thanking you for your inspiring words.

Thank you for talking at the funeral service for my aunt. The entire family appreciated your message and were happy that it included accepting Jesus as our Savior. Aunt [Name] was friends with many unsaved folks that came to the service. I hope your message had an impact on them.

We are thankful for the prayers and visits with [Child's Name]. The car accident was devastating. His injuries are starting to heal and should be able to come home soon. Thank you for being there for us and for him.

I love your teaching style! I can relate to your stories and how you weave in the Biblical messages. Thank you for agreeing to be our pastor! I am looking forward to learning more about Jesus through you.

Thank you for making the trip to the hospital to visit me when I had knee replacement surgery. I was feeling lonely and your presence lifted my spirit. The card you brought from the church was also very nice. I look forward to returning to church soon!

Thank you for all you do for the church! I see you every Sunday, but I've heard you are meeting with people and visiting them behind the scenes. The amount of support you provide is wonderful.

CHURCH MUSICIANS

MOST CHURCH SERVICES INCLUDE MUSIC. The musicians usually have spent years practicing to be able to play for you. Depending on the arrangements, some of the musicians may be unpaid volunteers. Next service, take a moment to thank them. If you want to stand out, hand them a thank-you note. However, most musicians would be thrilled to hear your kind words without a note.

What if you don't like your church's current music? If you have decided to not change churches because of the music, you can still thank them for their service. Also, remember that the music situation may be temporary. In the next year, the praise band could have a member switch up or the not so good organist may be replaced with an excellent organist.

Examples:

> *Thank you for playing for us each week. I enjoy your music.*
>
> *Your playing today inspired me to sing. Thank You.*
>
> *I appreciate how well you can play* [Instrument]. *Your talent amazes me each week!*

I look forward to the hymns every Sunday when you are at the organ. You are a master!

Your voice is wonderful. Thank you for blessing us each week.

Thank you for singing in the choir each week. The choir helps me sing along with the hymns. You are doing great leading your section.

The choir is amazing! I enjoy the programs you put together each week. The choir is lucky to have you as their director.

Thank you for leading us in song each week. (This one sentence is good even if you don't like the music—the person is still dedicating their time and effort to the church community.)

The choir's performance during the [Holiday] *service was impressive. Thank you for choosing such a great program! I love how you were able to integrate the organ.*

I enjoyed your trumpet solo! Thank you for taking the time to learn it as I know you are very busy with your day job.

CHURCH VOLUNTEERS

MOST CHURCHES RELY ON VOLUNTEERS to run their programs (Vacation Bible School, Sunday School, or other classes), to bring donuts and coffee, manage the nursery during services, perform minor maintenance, assist with the audio-visual equipment, etc. And in many churches, the 80/20 Rule seems to apply: 20% of the people are doing 80% of the work.

Thanking volunteers with a small gift or thank-you note will help them to know that their efforts are appreciated.

HOW TO SHOW YOUR APPRECIATION
TO CHURCH VOLUNTEERS:

- **Get the kids involved.** For children's programs, have the children make thank-you cards. They can use construction paper and write thank-you on them.

- **Pass out a small gift**, such as $5 or $10 gift cards to local coffee place or restaurant.

- **Say "thank you" as much as you can.** I always appreciate it when the parent(s) are picking up their child from the church nursery say, "thank you."

- **Look for ideas on Pinterest.** There will be many boards with ideas.

- **Get crafty.** Homemade items combined with a small gift seem to be popular.

- **Order food.** Have a pizza party after a church service to thank all the volunteers.

Examples:

Thank you for making the coffee each week! I look forward to having a cup each week. I appreciate the time you take to arrive early and having it ready.

My daughter loves your class! You've been made learning Bible verses easy for her. She tells us every detail of class during Sunday lunch.

Thank you for making the Bible stories fun for the six year olds. Our son is very engaged with your storytelling style and acts out the stories at home during the week. You are making an impact on him and his desire to learn more about the Bible and Jesus.

Your dedication to the nursery is wonderful. I feel at ease dropping off [Child's Name] when it's your week in the nursery. I appreciate the break and being able to focus on the worship and sermon.

VBS was great this year! Thank you for organizing the activities and having food for the volunteers beforehand was wonderful. The children I brought benefited from the program. One family has decided to join our church!

Thank you for running the PowerPoint Slides each week. The slides make it easier for me to take notes during the sermon and I know the younger generations appreciate having words to songs on the screen instead of looking a hymnal.

Thank you for donating your time and energy to paint the classrooms. They look so much better now and you saved the church from having to hire professional painters. Those funds will be dedicated elsewhere.

I want to thank you for organizing the meals that take place after a funeral. The families appreciate being able to have the funeral and the meal at the church. I have heard several people comment on how good the food is as well. The meal is a great way to help people with their grief by providing an environment for them to be able to share memories about their loved one.

I look forward to seeing your smile each Sunday when I arrive at church. I feel good knowing that no matter what I've been through during the week, you will be there on Sunday morning to greet as I come in. I can see how much you care for others in your eyes and that is very comforting. And my kids appreciate that you always remember their names! Thank you for volunteering to be a greeter.

Seeing someone notice a problem and then doing something about it is unusual! I noticed that you washed all the windows after overhearing others complain about how scuzzy and dirty they looked. They look so much better now. I admire your willingness to get things done!

VETERINARIAN

WHAT HAS YOUR VETERINARIAN DONE for you and your pets? Were the veterinarian and the office staff kind and comforting when your pet passed away?

Did the veterinarian help you in an emergency situation? When one of our cats mysteriously cut his leg, I was very thankful to find a 24-hour emergency veterinarian. Our current veterinarian would have helped any time of day!

Do you have a high maintenance pet? Is your veterinarian gentle and understanding with this pet? Does your veterinarian travel to your farm to see your horses or other farm animals?

I am grateful for having a great veterinarian. My cats have had several issues. He has been able to help them with treatment. He also advised us on how to make our house more cat-friendly when we went from owning three cats to owning six cats. If your veterinarian has provided you and your pet exceptional service, write them a handwritten thank-you note! The office staff can also be mentioned in the note.

Examples:

> *Thank you for all of the care you've provided for my dog, [Name] over the years. I want to thank you for being there for me and him when he got sick. It was a very sad and I appreciate the time you let me cry in the office.*

> *I appreciate you and the office staff. Helping the stray mom cat and her kittens has been more involved than I ever thought possible. Thank you for giving us the stray cat discount to get them all tested for the bad cat viruses. I am so relieved that they are all okay!*

> *I was worried when my cat lost so much weight. I am grateful that you were able to diagnosis her issue and start a treatment. I had no idea cats could have hyperactive thyroid! Thank you for being so thorough when explaining the various treatment options. This helped make my decision of choosing which treatment easier.*

> *I want to let you know how much I appreciate the staff at the office. They are friendly and always take time to answer my latest cat question. And they are very good about fitting in my cat at the last minute when they are sick.*

> *Thank you for figuring out what was wrong with [Pet's Name]! She had been so itchy lately. The allergy medicine is working already and she seems much more comfortable.*

> *Losing [Pet's Name] was very hard. Thank you for your support during the end of his life. Also, thanks for caring for him for the past fifteen years.*

> *Thank you for being willing to work with [Pet's Name]. He can be difficult to manage when he is scared. You seem to have the touch to calm him down. I appreciate*

your gentle and kind way with him as he responds well and is able to get his annual shots.

Thank you for coming to the farm when issues come up with the animals. I appreciate how far you travel and that the animals can be treated at the farm. Thanks again for your service. (Including a gas gift card in the note would be a nice touch!)

I am thankful that your office was able to squeeze in [Pet's Name] *on short notice. I had a feeling that the sore on her back had stopped healing. Thank you for confirming my suspicion! It has been two days and her back is already looking better! See you next week for the re-check.*

[Vet Tech/Receptionist's Name] *is full of knowledge. She is very helpful when I call in with questions about my cats. She has been able to provide advice over the phone that has kept me from needing to come in for an appointment. I am thankful that you have her on staff!*

PET GROOMER

THE PET GROOMER CAN MAKE YOUR PET look wonderful! My cat, Lina, has medium-length hair, and she was born without a tail. Sometimes her rear needs a shave!

If you are pleased with the job your pet groomer is doing, write them a handwritten thank-you note. The note can then be displayed at the pet drop-off area. This will let people know that the groomer is doing a good job.

You can also give your groomer a tip. I recommend thanking the groomer for whatever services they did for your pet and can include a compliment about how great your pet looks.

Examples:

> *Thank you for clipping* [Pet's Name] *nails. You are wonderful with him as he will not let me do it. He also looks great with his hair trimmed! I appreciate all you do to keep him looking good.*

> [Pet's Name] *always looks great after he's been with you! Thank you for taking the extra time to deal with his hair situation. He sheds so much this time of year.*

> *I appreciate the wonderful job you did removing the poo from* [Pet's Name]*'s hair. I don't understand why dogs*

roll around in it! He was a mess when he came home. I am so thankful that you were able to squeeze him in on short notice.

I love that I can depend on you to cut [Pet's Name]*'s nails. She is a lovely cat. She looks so pretty after you shampoo and brush her as well. Thank you for making her look more beautiful than ever!*

Thank you for your patience with [Pet's Name]. *I know that she can be quite the handful. I appreciate how gentle you are with her when washing her when she is attempting to escape. You are gift!*

[Pet's Name] *looks wonderful with her hair trimmed. Thank you for giving her a shampoo as well. I was also very surprised to see that you clipped her nails for no charge. That was very kind of you.*

I am very happy with how [Pet's Name] *looked after his visit with you! He looks so cute with his trimmed around his eyes. I am thankful that you have earned his trust. Thank you for all you do to make him look fantastic.*

Thanks for bending your same-day cash-only policy for me last week. I very rarely forgot to take my purse with me. Please enjoy this tip as I am very grateful that you did not make me reschedule.

I get so many compliments on [Pet's Name] *after you have groomed him! Your grooming skills make me look like the best pet owner ever. Thank you for helping me to show off how beautiful* [dog breed] *can be when properly groomed.*

Thank you for grooming [Pet's Name]. *Seeing her look so beautiful brings joy to my heart. Your services are worth every penny!*

PET SITTER

Having a reliable pet sitter makes it easier to go away and not have to worry about your pets.

My sister is my pet sitter when my husband and I go out of town. She checks on the cats, feeds them, scoops the litter boxes, spends time with them, and brings in the mail. That all takes time out of her day as she comes over at least twice a day.

What has your pet sitter done for you? Write them a handwritten thank-you note and leave it on the table for them to find during their first pet check. You can also send the note after you've returned from your trip.

Tips:

- **Even if you are paying the pet sitter, I still recommend a thank-you note.** Your money has compensated them for their time. Use your words to express your appreciation.

- **The note can be written as if the pets wrote it or from yourself.** Or you can write two notes—one from you and one from the pets.

Examples:

FROM THE PET

Thank you for feeding us while our human parents are away. We like to eat and have fresh water every day. We also like that you play with us and spend a little time talking to us.

We love it when you watch us. We look forward to the extra treats we get from you! Also, thanks for coming over twice a day to check on us. We normally sleep all day, but we like the attention.

I am glad that I don't have to be boarded while my [Your Name] is away. I like the walks you take me on and that you spend some time brushing me. And of course, I like eating every day!

Thank you for taking such good care of me. I will try to be a good cat when you give me my daily medicine. It's not so bad, but it makes me a little nervous. Thank you in advance for giving me treats afterward!

Thank you for visiting with me each day when [Your Name] was on vacation. I like the attention you give me and that you pet me each time you stop by. I love the extra treats you give me too! They can be our secret.

You are our favorite sitter! Thank you for being amazing and spending so much time with us while our humans are away. We also appreciate the extra treats you bring us!

FROM THE PET OWNER

Thank you for watching the dogs while we are away. It's a comfort knowing that they will be looked after and let out on a regular basis. I appreciate your willingness to stay at the house and bring in the mail too.

I am glad that you were once again around to watch my cats while I traveled. I feel like it's a lot to ask to have you scoop eleven litter boxes twice a day. The cats like to have clean boxes and they are much more likely to use it when the boxes are not full of "clumps."

We appreciate you for letting out the dogs during the day while we are away. I realize this requires you to get up extra early each morning. The dogs love spending time with you. And it's great that you take the time to walk them after work. They like routine!

Thank you for checking on my cats each day while I was on vacation. You understand how important they are to me. I appreciate that you took the extra time to hang out with them when you could as they sure do love attention.

Thank you for letting the dogs stay at your place. They would not do well at home alone. And they seem to enjoy spending time with your dog. I am glad they all get along okay.

I am grateful that you were once again willing to stop by and feed the lizards and snakes while I was out of town. Thank you for your dedication to my pets. I feel so much better going away knowing that they will have a consistent supply of food.

CONCLUSION

CONCLUSION

THANK YOU FOR READING THIS BOOK and learning more about thank-you notes. I hope that you now feel confident when writing your own notes in any situation.

Remember that, just like most things we learn, thank-you note writing gets easier with practice. I challenge you to develop the thank-you note writing habit. Aim to write a thank-you note within a few days of receiving a gift or anything for which you want to thank someone.

I'd love to hear from you! Please contact me at *heidi@ tonsofthanks.com* with any feedback or success stories. Also, please consider writing an honest review of the book on Amazon.

ACKNOWLEDGMENTS

THANK YOU AGAIN FOR READING MY FIRST BOOK! I hope you have found it helpful.

This book was made possible because of my mom. My thank-you note writing habit was started by my mom when was a child. She taught my siblings and me the importance of writing thank-you notes. Mom, I thank you for teaching me a valuable skill!

I would also like to thank my husband, Ted. He has been very encouraging and supportive throughout this project.

This book is here today because of the support I received from Camilla Kragius and her "Getting Stuff Done" program. She provided accountability that helped me to meet weekly goals for finishing the book.

And finally, I thank my editor, Ann Maynard, for the improvements she made to this book.

ABOUT THE AUTHOR

HEIDI BENDER HAS BEEN WRITING THANK-YOU NOTES for more than 30 years. She lives in Michigan with her husband and their six cats. Heidi likes to spend time playing the organ, reading, going for walks (not on the beach!), and cooking homemade meals.

For more thank-you note information, tips, and examples, please visit *www.tonsofthanks.com*. To learn more about Heidi visit *www.heidibender.com*.

Made in the USA
Middletown, DE
14 August 2018